SOUTHERN CALIFORNIA TRIVIA

SOUTHERN CALIFORNIA TRIVIA

COMPILED BY ERNIE & JILL COUCH

Rutledge Hill Press

513 THIRD AVE., S.   NASHVILLE, TENNESSEE 37210

Published by Rutledge Hill Press, Inc., 513 Third Avenue South, Nashville, Tennessee 37210

Typography by Bailey Typography, Inc.
Cover photography by Doug Brachey Photography
Color separation by Manning Camera Graphics
Book and cover design by Ernie Couch / Consultx

Library of Congress Cataloging-in-Publication Data
Couch, Ernie, 1949-
      Southern California trivia / compiled by Ernie & Jill Couch.
          p.   cm.
      ISBN 1-55853-045-2
      1. California, Southern—Miscellanea. 2. Questions and answers.
I. Couch, Jill, 1948-   II. Title.
F867.C76   1989   89-29824
979.4'9—dc20   CIP

Printed in the United States of America
1 2 3 4 5 6 7 8 — 94 93 92 91 90 89

PREFACE

When you mention Southern California, such words as beach, sun, palm trees, and oranges flash through most minds. Yet these words become somewhat superficial when one digs into the multifaceted character of the region. Southern California is comprised of a richly diversified land and people, along with colorful traditions and a compelling history. Captured within these pages are some of the highlights of this rich heritage, both the known and the not-so-well known.

Southern California Trivia is designed to be informative, educational, and entertaining. Most of all, we hope that reading this book will motivate you to learn about this great region.

—Ernie & Jill Couch

To
Walter S. Hern, III
and
the great people of Southern California

TABLE OF CONTENTS

GEOGRAPHY

CHAPTER ONE

Q. What is the only city on Santa Catalina Island?

A. Avalon.

---◆---

Q. Quakers who formed the Pickering Land and Water Company established what town in 1887?

A. Whittier.

---◆---

Q. Where is the largest flea market in California held?

A. Lancaster.

---◆---

Q. George Meeker started what subdivision in West Covina in 1941?

A. Sun Kist Village.

---◆---

Q. What southern California community is the birthplace of the Hell's Angels?

A. Fontana.

Q. Dairy Valley, incorporated in 1956, is in what county?

A. Los Angeles.

———✦———

Q. The name of what Tulare County town is made from reversing the syllables of its former name?

A. Denlin (from Linden).

———✦———

Q. Where was the "Western White House" during the Nixon administration?

A. San Clemente.

———✦———

Q. What southern California town is called the "Avocado Capital of the World?

A. Fallbrook.

———✦———

Q. What is the meaning of the San Diego Spanish placename El Cajon?

A. "The box."

———✦———

Q. What was the original Spanish name given to Los Angeles in September 1781?

A. El Pueblo de Nuestra Señora la Reina de Los Angeles de Porciuncula ("The Town of Our Lady the Queen of the Angels of Porciuncula").

———✦———

Q. What southern California city was named for a Los Angeles dentist?

A. Burbank (for Dr. David Burbank).

Q. What is the largest county in the contiguous United States?

A. San Bernardino.

———◆———

Q. What 1957 industrial development was established on undeveloped land in La Puente?

A. City of Industry.

———◆———

Q. Campo de Cahuenga, the house on the site where Mexican general Andres Pico surrendered to John Fremont, is in what southern California city?

A. Hollywood.

———◆———

Q. Chino derives its name from what 1841 land grant?

A. Santa Ana del Chino.

———◆———

Q. Covering 125,000 acres, what is the world's largest U.S. Marine Corps Amphibious training base?

A. Camp Pendleton.

———◆———

Q. By what name is state highway 18 through the San Bernardino Mountains known?

A. "Rim of the World Drive."

———◆———

Q. What town developed by Edgar Rice Burroughs in 1919 was a forerunner of Tarzana?

A. Runnymede.

Q. When sympathizers named the Alabama Hills after a Confederate ship, what name was given in retaliation to the mines near Independence?

A. Kearsarge (the Union cruiser that sunk the *Alabama*).

———◆———

Q. On July 1, 1988, what southern California community incorporated into a city of approximately 50 square miles?

A. Hesperia.

———◆———

Q. What was the first suburb of Los Angeles?

A. Angelino Heights.

———◆———

Q. The extreme heat in the Salton Sea basin led to the name of what Riverside County town?

A. Thermal.

———◆———

Q. By what previous American name was Terminal Island known?

A. Rattlesnake Island.

———◆———

Q. What California city was founded in the late 1850s by the Los Angeles Vineyard Society?

A. Anaheim.

———◆———

Q. In 1910 Bishop William M. Bell established what settlement for retired ministers of the Church of the United Brethren in Christ?

A. Otterbein.

Q. What southern California city bills itself as the "Gem of the Pacific Coast"?

A. Oceanside.

———◆———

Q. What is the meaning of the Spanish place-name, Cima?

A. "Summit."

———◆———

Q. Next to black, what is the most common color adjective used in California place-names?

A. Red.

———◆———

Q. Ortega Hill, which rises to a height of 4,970 feet, is in what southern California county?

A. Ventura.

———◆———

Q. In 1955 what was the fastest growing city in the United States?

A. West Covina.

———◆———

Q. What is the meaning of the Los Angeles County Spanish place-name of El Monte?

A. "The thicket."

———◆———

Q. McDonnell Douglas Corporation is headquartered in what southern California city?

A. Santa Monica.

Q. South Laguna was known by what name from 1933 to 1934?

A. Three Arches.

———◆———

Q. Square Mile Park is in what community?

A. Fountain Valley.

———◆———

Q. The California Lutheran College is in what community?

A. Thousand Oaks.

———◆———

Q. What Kern County town founded in 1914 was named in honor of the U.S. commander in Cuba during the Spanish-American War?

A. Shafer (for Gen. William "Pecos Bill" Shafer).

———◆———

Q. What was the first seat of Kern County?

A. Havilah.

———◆———

Q. The railroad junction that developed into Barstow was first called by what name?

A. Waterman.

———◆———

Q. What valley in Los Angeles County was named for a Basque sheepherder?

A. Leonis Valley (for Miquel Leonis).

GEOGRAPHY

Q. The Colorado River forms portions of the borders of what three southern California counties?

A. San Bernardino, Riverside, and Imperial.

———✦———

Q. Indiana Colony evolved into what southern California city?

A. Pasadena.

———✦———

Q. In 1911 what name was applied to Standard Oil Company's second California refinery and the community nearby?

A. El Segundo.

———✦———

Q. What Indian reservation is situated just north and east of Warner Springs?

A. Los Coyotes.

———✦———

Q. The communities of Edgmont, Sunnymead, and Moreno incorporated into what city on December 3, 1984?

A. Moreno Valley.

———✦———

Q. Where is the home of Pepperdine University?

A. Malibu.

———✦———

Q. For what 1863 settler was Bakersfield named?

A. Colonel Thomas Baker.

Q. What Tulare County mountain was named in the 1870s for a local school teacher?

A. Mount Maggie (for Maggie Kincaid).

———◆———

Q. The Los Angeles County community of Walnut was known by what name before 1912?

A. Lemon.

———◆———

Q. In land area, what is the smallest county in southern California?

A. Orange.

———◆———

Q. Weed Patch is in what southern California county?

A. Kern.

———◆———

Q. What California town sits directly across the border from Mexicali, Mexico?

A. Calexico.

———◆———

Q. Founded in 1927, Los Angeles Baptist College is in what community?

A. Newhall.

———◆———

Q. In 1887 H. A. Palmer declined the offer to have what Los Angeles County town named in his honor?

A. Claremont.

Q. What is the fourth largest predominantly black municipality in the United States?

A. Compton.

———◆———

Q. El Centro is the seat of what county?

A. Imperial.

———◆———

Q. During the late 1870s, what Los Angeles County town was founded by a well drilling firm?

A. Artesia (by the Artesia Company).

———◆———

Q. Where is the longest, highest, and only solid concrete municipal pier in the United States?

A. Huntington Beach (constructed in 1914).

———◆———

Q. By what name was Carlsbad first known?

A. Frazier's Station.

———◆———

Q. What community bears the motto "Freeway City" on its official seal?

A. Gardena.

———◆———

Q. What was the former name of Edwards Air Force Base?

A. Muroc Air Field.

Q. Westmont College is in what city?

A. Santa Barbara.

———◆———

Q. The offices of the Auditor General of the Air Force and the Deputy Inspector for Inspection and World Safety are at what military base?

A. Norton Air Force Base.

———◆———

Q. On what Channel Island is Smugglers' Cove?

A. Santa Cruz Island.

———◆———

Q. What community in the southeastern corner of San Bernardino County is named for a Canadian city?

A. Ontario.

———◆———

Q. In what community may the Mission Revival-style Holt House and the Queen Anne-style Morey House be seen?

A. Redlands.

———◆———

Q. Founded in 1887, what is the oldest of the six Claremont Colleges?

A. Pomona College.

———◆———

Q. In 1957 what southern California city was featured by *Look* magazine as an "All-American City"?

A. Torrance.

Q. By what previous name was Watts known?

A. Mud Town.

———◆———

Q. Where is the Water Softening and Filtration Plant of Metropolitan Water District of Southern California?

A. La Verne (built in 1940).

———◆———

Q. In 1910 what town was renamed Erp in honor of the frontier peace officer Wyatt Earp?

A. Drennan.

———◆———

Q. What Air Force base leads all others in the nation for the number of clear flying days?

A. George Air Force Base.

———◆———

Q. What is the highest of the mountain ranges that surround Los Angeles?

A. San Bernardino Mountains.

———◆———

Q. What is the meaning of the Spanish place-name Sierra Madre?

A. "Mother range."

———◆———

Q. Prior to 1927, the community of Agoura in Los Angeles County was known by what name?

A. Picture City.

Q. What Riverside County town grew up around a store built by Procco Akimo in 1872?

A. San Jacinto.

———◆———

Q. Both in area and in population, what is the largest city in California?

A. Los Angeles.

———◆———

Q. What 1906 subdivision was later renamed Monterey Park?

A. Romona Acres.

———◆———

Q. The construction of a beet-sugar refinery in 1897 led to the establishment of what Ventura County town?

A. Oxnard.

———◆———

Q. For whom was Holy Jim Canyon in Orange County named?

A. James ("Cussin' Jim") Smith.

———◆———

Q. Where is the 200-foot California Tower situated?

A. Balboa Park, San Diego.

———◆———

Q. From what two counties was Kern County created on April 2, 1866?

A. Los Angeles and Tulare.

Q. "Where the Sun Spends the Winter" is the motto of what southern California town?

A. El Centro.

———◆———

Q. What California city developed on the former site of the Yokuts Indian Village of Way Loo?

A. Bakersfield.

———◆———

Q. What was the name of Manhattan Beach prior to 1902?

A. Shore Acres.

———◆———

Q. The Cahuilla Indian Reservation is south of what community?

A. Anza.

———◆———

Q. What was the original name of Compton?

A. Gibsonville.

———◆———

Q. What Riverside County town founded in 1884 was named for a stagecoach line operator?

A. Banning (for Phineas Banning).

———◆———

Q. What California city is the home of the Brooks Institute?

A. Santa Barbara.

Q. Sutil Island was formerly known by what name?

A. Gull Island.

———✦———

Q. Kern County covers how many square miles?

A. 8,065.

———✦———

Q. In Los Angeles County what mountain honors the name of a World War I soldier who died in France?

A. Mount Mooney (for John L. Mooney).

———✦———

Q. What two southern California counties share borders with Mexico?

A. San Diego and Imperial.

———✦———

Q. Because of the narrow gauge tracks, what nickname was given to the Carson and Colorado Railroad?

A. The Slim Princess.

———✦———

Q. Due to wind erosion, San Nicolas Island is known by what other name?

A. Passing Island.

———✦———

Q. When construction commenced in 1917, Savage Dam in San Diego County was given what name?

A. Lower Otay Dam.

Q. In 1873 what town did the Southern Pacific Railroad lay out two miles north of the Bakersfield business district?

A. Sumner (later called Kern or Kern City).

---◆---

Q. Blythe is situated in what valley?

A. Palo Verde.

---◆---

Q. In 1874 George Hansen laid out what town that bears the same name as a Moorish fort in Spain?

A. Alhambra.

---◆---

Q. What name is given to the section of Sunset Boulevard that runs through the western part of Hollywood?

A. Sunset Strip.

---◆---

Q. What community is the home of Dr. Robert Schuller's Crystal Cathedral?

A. Garden Grove.

---◆---

Q. Horace H. Wilcox laid out and named what southern California city in 1886?

A. Hollywood.

---◆---

Q. Covering 932 square miles, what is the world's largest U.S. Marine Corps Base?

A. Marine Corps Air Guard Combat Center.

Q. Prior to 1956, what was the name of Tierra del Sol?

A. Hipass.

------◆------

Q. Where is the largest privately owned airport in the nation?

A. Upland (owned by Cable Airport).

------◆------

Q. Irwindale was the first name of what present-day community?

A. West Covina.

------◆------

Q. What U.S. president is said to have suggested the name of Beverly Hills?

A. William Howard Taft.

------◆------

Q. In 1868 the city fathers of San Diego set aside what 1,400-acre tract "to be forever a public park"?

A. Balboa Park.

------◆------

Q. What mountain in Los Angeles County was named in honor of California's governor from 1891 to 1895?

A. Mount Markham (for Henry H. Markham).

------◆------

Q. During the 1870s and 1880s, what became the first "oil town" in Kings County?

A. Kettleman.

Q. A fancied resemblance to P. T. Barnum's famous elephant led to the name of what promontory in Linda Vista hills in 1884?

A. Jumbo Knob.

———◆———

Q. Founded in 1880, what is the oldest town in the Santa Ynez Valley?

A. Ballard.

———◆———

Q. Ole Hanson, one-time mayor of Seattle, created what prime real estate development in the mid-1920s?

A. San Clemente.

———◆———

Q. Antelope Valley College is in what community?

A. Lancaster.

———◆———

Q. In addition to silver, what two metals did the Cerro Gordo region supply to U.S. industry?

A. Zinc and lead.

———◆———

Q. The Port of Los Angeles is on what bay?

A. San Pedro.

———◆———

Q. What high promontory shelters San Diego Bay from the Pacific Ocean?

A. Point Loma.

Q. What San Diego County community is known as "Village by the Sea"?

A. Carlsbad.

◆

Q. A snail found by a visiting scientist in 1872 led to what California place-name?

A. Mount Helix (for *Helix aspersia*).

◆

Q. Plaster City is in the southwestern portion of what county?

A. Imperial.

◆

Q. Winterhaven is surrounded by what Indian reservation?

A. Fort Yuma Indian Reservation.

◆

Q. The old Circle C Ranch in San Bernardino County became what residential development around 1924?

A. Wrightwood.

◆

Q. What Inyo County Canyon was named for a native of the Isle of Man?

A. Watterson Canyon (for George Watterson).

◆

Q. According to the Danish Rock monument in Solvang Park, what is the distance between Solvang and Copenhagen?

A. 11,270 kilometers.

Q. The merger of Hayes and Clearwater in 1948 formed what new community?

A. Paramount.

———◆———

Q. What southern California town was named for the tenth president of the Santa Fe Railroad?

A. Barstow (for William Barstow Strong).

———◆———

Q. In 1888 H. L. Williams laid out what town along the Santa Barbara to Ventura section of the Southern Pacific Railroad?

A. Summerland.

———◆———

Q. The annexation of what area by Chula Vista in 1985 set a California record for population added to a city?

A. Montgomery.

———◆———

Q. Harry H. Culver, for whom Culver City is named, came to southern California from what state in 1914?

A. Nebraska.

———◆———

Q. In what city did Fra Junipero Serra build the first of his twenty-one missions?

A. San Diego (The Mission San Diego de Alcala).

———◆———

Q. What is the highest peak in the Mojave Desert?

A. Clark Mountain (7,929 feet).

Q. What hiking trail, not yet complete, will eventually run the length of California north to south?

A. The Pacific Crest Trail.

———◆———

Q. In what California city was Richard Nixon born?

A. Yorba Linda.

———◆———

Q. When Wells Fargo refused to ship silver from Panamint City, what solution did Senator William Stewart devise?

A. He shipped it in 750 pound balls, too heavy to steal.

———◆———

Q. What city was once called "nineteen suburbs in search of a city"?

A. Los Angeles.

———◆———

Q. When Willmore City went bankrupt in 1888, it recovered by advertising itself as a sea resort with what new name?

A. Long Beach.

———◆———

Q. The California Baptist College is situated in what city?

A. Riverside.

———◆———

Q. What Pasadena landmark was used as an Army hospital during World War II?

A. The Vista del Arroy Hotel and Bungalows.

Q. In what community is the largest growth of bougainvillea in the continental U.S.?

A. Glendora.

———◆———

Q. What was the last California fort established by the Spanish?

A. The Santa Barbara Presidio (April 1872).

———◆———

Q. According to legend, goat's milk was mixed into the mortar of what resort hotel to provide added strength?

A. The Zane Grey Pueblo Hotel (Santa Catalina Island).

———◆———

Q. What is the only remaining Civil War landmark in California?

A. The Drum Barracks in Wilmington.

———◆———

Q. What was the first hotel in America built specifically for blacks?

A. The Somerville (Dunbar) Hotel, Wilmington.

———◆———

Q. Of the eleven remaining covered bridges in the state, where is the only one in southern California?

A. Felton.

———◆———

Q. What community, called the "Chautauqua of the West," was founded as a Methodist summer camp?

A. Pacific Grove.

Q. How many rooms did the Winchester Mystery House originally have?

A. Eight (now 160).

———◆———

Q. In what community did the first "jail" consist of a chain attached to a large tree?

A. Sonora.

———◆———

Q. What fault is responsible for the formation of the El Paso Mountains?

A. The Garlock Fault.

———◆———

Q. What community is known as the "Gateway to the Mojave"?

A. Barstow.

———◆———

Q. What county tried to ban John Steinbeck's *The Grapes of Wrath* because of the way it depicted California's treatment of Okies?

A. Kern.

———◆———

Q. Construction on what man-made harbor was begun in April 1899?

A. San Pedro (in Los Angeles).

———◆———

Q. Of the 25 million acres of California desert, how much is public land?

A. Approximately 15 million.

Q. What southern California national forest includes the Cucamonga, San Gorgonio, Santa Rosa and San Jacinto wilderness areas?

A. San Bernardino National Forest.

———◆———

Q. In what year was the Los Angeles Aqueduct, the system that brings water from Owens Lake, completed?

A. 1913.

———◆———

Q. Between what two cities did the narrow-gauge Carson and Colorado Railroad run?

A. Carson City, Nevada, and Keeler (then called Hawley), California.

———◆———

Q. What river valley is sometimes called "The Land of Little Rain"?

A. Owens Valley.

———◆———

Q. In what city did Dr. Francis Townsend first win support for his old age pension movement?

A. Long Beach.

———◆———

Q. Calteck Peak is in what county?

A. Tulare.

———◆———

Q. The mansion used for the exteriors of Tara in *Gone With The Wind* actually overlooked what community?

A. Culver City.

Q. What Orange County city's name was suggested by T. E. Schmidt in 1858?

A. Anaheim.

———✦———

Q. A local legend states that the gold of a Spanish galleon is buried beneath the sand dunes near what city?

A. Kane Springs.

———✦———

Q. What town, originally named Paringa, was moved after the completion of the Southern Pacific Railroad survey?

A. Heber.

———✦———

Q. What Southern California landmark was once described as "a first step toward Heaven"?

A. Forest Lawn Memorial Park.

———✦———

Q. What twin cities were named by combining syllables from "Mexico" and "California"?

A. Calexico and Mexicali.

———✦———

Q. By what nickname is the Lucerne Valley often called?

A. "Crossroads of the Desert."

———✦———

Q. What was the first Los Angeles house designed by Frank Lloyd Wright?

A. Hollyhock House, Barnsdall Park.

Q. What Spanish-named highway first connected the southern California mission towns?

A. El Camino Real.

———◆———

Q. In which of his missions did Fra Junipero Serra die?

A. Mission San Carlos Borromeo (Carmel).

———◆———

Q. What Tulare County community was founded, financed, and governed by black Americans?

A. Allensworth.

———◆———

Q. In what California desert are tracks left by General Patton's tanks in the 1940s still visible?

A. The Colorado (Sonoran) region.

———◆———

Q. During the silver strike, where did silver bars pile up so fast that workers built houses out of them?

A. Cerro Gordo.

———◆———

Q. What dam on the Owens River was built to divert water to the Los Angeles Aqueduct?

A. Tinemaha.

———◆———

Q. Along what U.S. Highway can scarp from the 1872 earthquake be seen?

A. U.S. 395.

Q. What Death Valley mining town was named for a popular slang expression?

A. Skidoo.

———◆———

Q. From the trail up what mountain can both the lowest and highest points of the contiguous 48 states be seen?

A. Telescope Peak (from Death Valley to Mount Whitney).

———◆———

Q. The second largest city in San Diego County bears what Spanish name meaning "beautiful view"?

A. Chula Vista.

———◆———

Q. In what city did Aimee Semple McPherson build her Church of the Four-Square Gospel?

A. Los Angeles.

———◆———

Q. What city is the oldest Spanish settlement in California?

A. San Diego.

———◆———

Q. What valley was the setting for Harold Bell Wright's novel, *The Winning of Barbara Worth?*

A. Imperial Valley.

———◆———

Q. What national monument, called a geologist's paradise, contains rock from every great division of geologic time?

A. Death Valley National Monument.

Q. In 1910 what San Diego hotel was established by a U.S. President's son?

A. The U. S. Grant Hotel (established by Ulysses S. Grant, Jr.).

———◆———

Q. What is the only fresh water body in southern California?

A. Lake Elsinore.

———◆———

Q. The turn-of-the-century popularity of Queen Anne and Mission Revival architecture can be partially traced to what Riverside landmark?

A. The Mission Inn.

———◆———

Q. What U.S. Army fort was home of the experimental "Camel Corps," 1857-61?

A. Fort Tejon (near Lebec).

———◆———

Q. What was the first permanent European settlement on the Pacific Coast?

A. The San Diego Presidio.

———◆———

Q. At what university did seismologist Charles Richter devise the scale for measuring the strength of earthquakes?

A. California Institute of Technology.

———◆———

Q. The first white man to explore California came in search of what mythical region?

A. Cibola and its seven cities of gold.

Q. What California desert is a tropical desert, literally a jungle that dried up?

A. The Colorado (Sonoran).

———◆———

Q. What bowl-shaped depression near Pearlblossom resulted from the nearby San Andreas and San Jacinto faults?

A. The Devil's Punchbowl.

———◆———

Q. What Los Angeles shopping mall, built in the Streamline Moderne style, has been declared a historic monument?

A. Crossroads of the World.

———◆———

Q. Where are the most outstanding tufa towers in the U.S.?

A. The Pinnacles National Natural Landmark.

———◆———

Q. What San Diego landmark was built by Jesse Shepard, also known as the writer Francis Grierson?

A. Villa Montezuma.

———◆———

Q. What fault caused the 1872 earthquake?

A. The Alabama Hills fault.

———◆———

Q. What city is located on part of the Rancho San Rafael, the first Spanish land grant in California (1784)?

A. Glendale.

Q. What community was once known for its inadequate horse-car line, the "Get Off and Push Railroad"?

A. Willmore City, now Long Beach.

Q. In which community can you take the walking "Red Tile Tour" of historic sites?

A. Santa Barbara.

Q. The elephant tree, a desert plant, is found only in what desert region?

A. The Anza-Borrego.

Q. What mineral mined from the desert has resulted in more wealth than either silver or gold?

A. Borax.

Q. What mine in the West Panamint Valley provided George Hearst $2 million of silver ore, starting the Hearst fortune?

A. The Modoc mine.

Q. Norma Talmadge accidentally created a tradition when she stepped in wet cement in front of what Hollywood monument?

A. Mann's Chinese Theatre (formerly Grauman's).

Q. What was the first frame building in Death Valley?

A. A miner's boarding house, which now houses the Borax Museum.

Q. What peak in the Santa Anna Mountains was named for the Polish actress who organized a colony for refugee Polish artists in 1876?

A. Modjeska (for Mme. Helene Modjeska).

———◆———

Q. What famous "cave" is not really a cave, but a large hollow in a huge boulder?

A. Smuggler's Cave.

———◆———

Q. Where is the Pegleg Smith Monument, the site of a Liar's Contest each April?

A. Anza-Borrego Desert State Park.

———◆———

Q. What section of Los Angeles is called "the Miracle Mile"?

A. Wilshire Boulevard, from Vermont to La Brea.

———◆———

Q. What is the total weight of the 45-foot high letters of the "Hollywood" sign?

A. 480,000 pounds.

———◆———

Q. Once the backlot of Twentieth Century-Fox studios, Century City was originally part of what film star's ranch?

A. Tom Mix.

———◆———

Q. In what community is Rancho Alamitos, California's oldest standing Spanish ranch, situated?

A. Long Beach.

Q. What is California's largest offshore island?

A. Santa Cruz.

———◆———

Q. What rock formation has been called Los Angeles' most distinctive natural landmark?

A. Eagle Rock.

———◆———

Q. What city park contains a greater variety of trees than any other park of its size in North America?

A. MacArthur Park, Los Angeles.

———◆———

Q. What city is the home to the largest fig tree in North America?

A. Santa Barbara.

———◆———

Q. Where is the "Oak of the Golden Dream," location of the southern California gold rush that started in 1842?

A. Placerita Canyon State Park.

———◆———

Q. In what community is a portion of Mahatma Gandhi's ashes located?

A. Pacific Palisades (at the Self-Realization Fellowship Lake Shrine).

———◆———

Q. In and around what community do millions of monarch butterflies spend the winter?

A. Ventura.

Q. In what southern California county is the world's largest undisturbed pavement plain, a 124-acre surface of clay and saragossa quartz?

A. San Bernardino County Big Bear Valley Preserve.

———◆———

Q. Chino derives its name from what 1841 land grant?

A. Santa Ana del Chino.

———◆———

Q. In what zoo was the first California condor successfully born in captivity?

A. San Diego Zoo.

———◆———

Q. In what Pacific Ocean cove can a cave in the sandstone bluff be reached through a store?

A. La Jolla (The La Jolla Cave and Shell Shop).

———◆———

Q. The Festival of Whales, where the southward migration of gray whales is monitored, is at what marine attraction?

A. The Orange County Marine Institute, Dana Point Harbor.

———◆———

Q. What park was created when fossil beds were exposed when sand and gravel was dug out to build freeways?

A. The Ralph B. Clark Regional Park, north Orange County.

———◆———

Q. What dry lake bed has recently become a marsh due to irrigation run-off from neighboring farms?

A. Harper Dry Lake, Barstow.

Q. What house built by Henry and Charles Greene is now a library and research center devoted to their work?

A. The Gamble House, Pasadena.

———◆———

Q. What is the only house in Pasadena designed by Frank Lloyd Wright?

A. The Millard House.

———◆———

Q. Where is the *Star of India,* the oldest floating iron-hulled merchantman, berthed?

A. The San Diego Maritime Museum.

———◆———

Q. What is the oldest fired-brick building in San Bernardino County?

A. The John Rains house, Rancho Cucamonga.

———◆———

Q. What Los Angeles church is a branch of the Mission San Gabriel Arcangel?

A. The Church of Our Lady of All Angels.

———◆———

Q. What was the former name of Hobo Hot Springs in Kern County?

A. Clear Creek Hot Springs.

———◆———

Q. What was the first name of Glendale?

A. Riverdale.

Q. In 1931 the town of Osdick received what new name?

A. Red Mountain.

———◆———

Q. The Pico Oak, with a trunk that forms an arch, is in what valley?

A. The Santa Clarita.

———◆———

Q. Erected in 1928, the "Hollywood" sign was originally an advertisement for what company?

A. Hollywoodland Realty.

———◆———

Q. Two plants endemic to California—the giant coreopsis and the live-forever—reach their southern limit at what state park?

A. Point Dume State Beach.

———◆———

Q. What park is headquarters of the Tree People, an organization that plants smog-resistant trees?

A. Coldwater Canyon.

———◆———

Q. What southern California home is considered the second most opulent house west of the Mississippi?

A. Doheny's Greystone Mansion, Beverly Hills.

———◆———

Q. What California park was the site of the 1932 Olympics?

A. Los Angeles' Exposition Park.

ENTERTAINMENT

C H A P T E R   T W O

Q. What Los Angeles-born actor made his film debut in *Red Sky at Morning*, 1972?

A. Desi Arnaz, Jr.

———◆———

Q. What Hollywood-born actor directed the 1981 film *Tarzan, the Ape Man?*

A. John Derek.

———◆———

Q. How old was Los Angeles native Richie Valens when he was killed in a North Iowa airplane crash?

A. 17.

———◆———

Q. Who made up the duo of Jan and Dean?

A. Jan Berry and Dean Torrence.

———◆———

Q. "Marcus Welby, M.D." was set in what southern California city?

A. Santa Monica.

Q. Where is the annual W. C. Fields Festival held?

A. Ryon Park, Lompac.

———◆———

Q. What is the actual name of Cheech, of Cheech and Chong fame?

A. Richard Marin.

———◆———

Q. What is Cher's actual name?

A. Cherilyn Sakasian La Pierre.

———◆———

Q. Los Angeles actress Elizabeth Montgomery starred in what 1964-72 TV sit-com?

A. "Bewitched."

———◆———

Q. What southern California native starred in "The Life and Times of Grizzly Adams"?

A. Dan Haggerty.

———◆———

Q. What Santa Barbara-born actor was best known for his roles in "Little House on the Prairie," "Carter Country," and "Highway to Heaven"?

A. Victor French.

———◆———

Q. What Hawthorne group was first known by such names as Carl and the Passions, Kenny and the Cadets, and the Pendletones?

A. The Beach Boys.

Q. Writer/director Roger Beatty received five Emmys for what TV show?

A. "The Carol Burnett Show" (1972, 1973, 1974, 1975, 1978).

———◆———

Q. In 1921 what popular silent movie Western star purchased the 300-acre Horseshoe Ranch in Newhall?

A. William S. Hart.

———◆———

Q. What Glendale native appeared in *The Land That Time Forgot, At the Earth's Core, Warlords of Atlantis,* and *Humanoids from the Deep?*

A. Doug McClure.

———◆———

Q. In 1979 what single reached No. 4 for Los Angeles native Rickie Lee Jones?

A. "Chuck E's in Love."

———◆———

Q. Where was actor Gregory Harrison born on May 31, 1950?

A. Avalon.

———◆———

Q. Jackie Cooper starred in what NBC show with a dog named Cleo?

A. "The People's Choice."

———◆———

Q. What Hollywood-born actress co-starred with Larry Hagman in the short-lived 1973 TV series, "Here We Go Again"?

A. Diane Baker.

Q. Where did Beach Boys' drummer Dennis Wilson drown in 1983?

A. Marina Del Rey.

———◆———

Q. Who coined the name "Melody Ranch" and later purchased the movie ranch owned by Monogram Pictures' Ernie Hickson?

A. Gene Autry.

———◆———

Q. What is actress Terry Moore's actual name?

A. Helen Koford.

———◆———

Q. What actor starred with Richard O'Brien in the 1982 film, *Shock Treatment?*

A. Cliff DeYoung.

———◆———

Q. What do the initials in A & M Records stand for?

A. Herb Alpert and John Moss.

———◆———

Q. Carl Gardner and Bobby Nunn, original members of The Coasters, came out of what Los Angeles rhythm and blues group?

A. The Robins.

———◆———

Q. What Pasadena-born musician is part of the singing duo The Captain and Tennille?

A. Daryl Dragon.

Q. Although she had appeared in short films since age 3, in what movie did Shirley Temple make her feature debut?

A. *Red Haired Alibi* (1932).

---◆---

Q. What Los Angeles-born actress appeared in *American Hot Wax* but gained national attention on "Saturday Night Live"?

A. Loraine Newman.

---◆---

Q. What power/pop quintet was formed in 1977?

A. The Motels.

---◆---

Q. What epic silent movie was shot on the ranch of David W. Griffith?

A. *Birth of a Nation.*

---◆---

Q. On what TV series did Kent McCord begin his acting career?

A. "Ozzie and Harriet Show."

---◆---

Q. Where was Jim Messina born on December 5, 1947?

A. Maywood.

---◆---

Q. Los Angeles native Nick Benedict played what character on the TV serial "All My Children"?

A. Phillip Brent.

Q. Where was drummer Sandy Nelson born in 1938?

A. Santa Monica.

———◆———

Q. To what nation did Shirley Temple Black serve as U.S. Ambassador, 1974-76?

A. Ghana.

———◆———

Q. What dance of the 1930s originated at the Balboa Pavilion at Newport Beach?

A. The "Balboa Hop."

———◆———

Q. What Los Angeles rock group was formed in 1965 by Arthur Lee?

A. Love (first called Grass Roots).

———◆———

Q. In what movie did actress Margaret O'Brien make her screen debut at age four?

A. *Babes in Arms.*

———◆———

Q. On April 1, 1963, Los Angeles native John Beradino began playing what character on "General Hospital"?

A. Steve Hardy, Director of Medicine.

———◆———

Q. What southern California native played Dolly Pelliker in the 1983 movie *Silkwood?*

A. Cher.

Q. Los Angeles-born Randy Newman had what No. 2 single in 1978?

A. "Short People."

———◆———

Q. What San Diego native has appeared in *Freaky Friday, Big Wednesday, Sweater Girl,* and *The New Centurions?*

A. Charlene Tilton.

———◆———

Q. What musical event is held each November at Wilard?

A. Old time Fiddlers Contest.

———◆———

Q. By what former name was the Nitty Gritty Dirt Band known?

A. Illegitimate Jug Band.

———◆———

Q. What singer had a 1981 No. 1 hit single with "Bette Davis Eyes"?

A. Kim Carnes.

———◆———

Q. For what 1971 movie did San Bernardino-born Gene Hackman receive an Oscar for Best Actor?

A. *The French Connection.*

———◆———

Q. For what 1973 movie did Tatum O'Neal receive an Oscar as Best Supporting Actress?

A. *Paper Moon.*

Q. For what actor was Orange County Airport renamed?

A. John Wayne.

Q. In what year did guitarist and vocalist Ry Cooder release his first album on Reprise?

A. 1970.

Q. Where was Bonnie Raitt born on November 8, 1947?

A. Los Angeles.

Q. Santa Barbara-born Chris Bernau played Alan Spaulding in what TV soap opera?

A. "The Guiding Light."

Q. What Los Angeles-born actress has won Tonys for her roles in "Can Can," "Damn Yankees," "New Girl in Town," and "Redhead"?

A. Gwen Verdon.

Q. Los Angeles-born actor Joel McCrea played a drifter in what two-fisted 1935 movie drama?

A. *Barbary Coast.*

Q. What was the original name of the Go Gos?

A. Misfits.

Q. In the 1930s what Thousand Oaks landmark was used in the filming of a Western starring Hoot Gibson and Sally Eilers?

A. Grand Union Hotel (Stagecoach Inn).

———◆———

Q. Where was Gregory Peck born on April 5, 1916?

A. La Jolla.

———◆———

Q. San Diego-born Tony Bill received an Oscar for producing what Best Picture of 1973?

A. *The Sting.*

———◆———

Q. Mary Cathleen Collins is the original name of what Long Beach-born actress?

A. Bo Derek.

———◆———

Q. What 1962 movie netted Gregory Peck an Oscar?

A. *To Kill a Mockingbird.*

———◆———

Q. Where was *Shootout at the OK Corral* filmed?

A. Morongo Valley (Pioneertown).

———◆———

Q. What southern California cowboy was the first Western film star to begin a TV series?

A. Gene Autry ("The Gene Autry Show").

Q. Los Angeles-born Eric Jones joined what multi-national musical group in 1975?

A. Heatwave.

———◆———

Q. Which of the Righteous Brothers duo was born in Los Angeles in 1940?

A. Bill Medley.

———◆———

Q. Who provided the voice for Mickey Mouse?

A. Walt Disney.

———◆———

Q. What was The Beach Boys' first release on Capitol?

A. "Surfin' Safari" (1962).

———◆———

Q. In 1979 what southern Californian won an Oscar for her performance in the film *Norma Rae?*

A. Sally Field.

———◆———

Q. What was the title of Jan and Dean's first album?

A. "Dead Man's Curve."

———◆———

Q. Where is the Roy Rogers and Dale Evans Museum?

A. Victorville.

Q. In what 1960 film did actress Yvette Mimieux make her screen debut?

A. *Platinum High School.*

Q. In what year did the Tijuana Brass disband?

A. 1969.

Q. What 1950s sit-com was built around the theme of an advice-to-the-lovelorn columnist for a Los Angeles newspaper?

A. "Dear Phoebe."

Q. Who succeeded Stanley Andrews as host of the TV series "Death Valley Days"?

A. Ronald Reagan.

Q. What unusual 1958 documentary TV series centered around couples discussing marital problems?

A. "Divorce Hearing."

Q. Who played hard-working Sergeant Joe Friday in the long-running "Dragnet" TV series?

A. Jack Webb.

Q. The 1984 TV series "The Duck Factory" used what type of small, struggling Hollywood firm for its setting?

A. A cartoon studio.

Q. What 1972-77 TV series depicted two paramedics with Squad 51 of the Los Angeles County Fire Department?

A. "Emergency."

———◆———

Q. Who were the first hosts of the Los Angeles-based "Entertainment Tonight"?

A. Tom Hallick, Marjorie Wallace, and Rod Hendren.

———◆———

Q. In what year did TV personality Ernie Kovacs die in an auto accident while driving home after a Beverly Hills party?

A. 1962.

———◆———

Q. What was the large Los Angeles-based conglomerate in the TV series, "Executive Suite"?

A. Cardway Corporation.

———◆———

Q. What southern California city was the setting for the TV drama series, "Family"?

A. Pasadena.

———◆———

Q. Who interviewed celebrities on the daytime TV series, "Dateline: Hollywood"?

A. Joanna Barnes.

———◆———

Q. What undercover Los Angeles police officer did David Cassidy play in "David Cassidy—Man Under Cover"?

A. Officer Dan Shay.

Q. Though first aired locally in Los Angeles, in what year did "Day in Court" go on network TV?

A. 1958.

———◆———

Q. Where did John Belushi and Dan Aykroyd do their first live gig in 1978 as the Blue Brothers?

A. Universal Amphitheatre in Los Angeles.

———◆———

Q. What hit single did the Nitty Gritty Dirt Band have in 1970?

A. "Mr. Bojangles."

———◆———

Q. What Los Angeles-born director won a 1981 Emmy for "Hill Street Blues"?

A. Robert Butler.

———◆———

Q. What 1937 classic by Walt Disney's studio was the first full-length cartoon movie?

A. *Snow White and the Seven Dwarfs.*

———◆———

Q. What Maywood actress appeared in *The Heretic, Beyond the Bermuda Triangle,* and *California Suite?*

A. Dana Plato.

———◆———

Q. What 1983 movie was centered around a Los Angeles police unit with a specially equipped helicopter?

A. *Blue Thunder.*

Q. Life at Hollywood Century Studios was the theme for what TV series?

A. "Bracken's World."

———◆———

Q. What San Diego private eye did Rod Cameron play in the 1959 TV series "Coronado 9"?

A. Dan Adams.

———◆———

Q. Jack Webb produced what early 1970s half-hour series with Robert Conrad as Deputy District Attorney Paul Ryan?

A. "The D.A."

———◆———

Q. What Warner Brothers Saturday morning cartoon show first aired in 1978?

A. "The Daffy Duck Show."

———◆———

Q. What record by Three Dog Night was the No. 1 single for 1971?

A. "Joy to the World."

———◆———

Q. Who hosted the Los Angeles-based dance contest show, "Dance Fever"?

A. Deney Terrio.

———◆———

Q. Howard Duff played Detective Sam Stone in what crime show set in Los Angeles?

A. "Felony Squad."

Q. In what decade was the private eye series "City of Angels" set?

A. 1930s.

───◆───

Q. In 1960 what became the first daytime soap opera to originate from Hollywood?

A. "The Clear Horizon."

───◆───

Q. What dramatic anthology series was presented in the "Hollywood Television Theatre" from November 1973 through January 1974?

A. "Conflicts."

───◆───

Q. What informative show for consumers hosted by David Horowitz first originated locally in Los Angeles?

A. "Consumer Buyline."

───◆───

Q. In what year did Buffalo Springfield form in Los Angeles?

A. 1966.

───◆───

Q. Red Rock Canyon, which has served as the set of many Western movies, is situated near what community?

A. Cantil.

───◆───

Q. What Los Angeles-born actor was originally named Francis Timothy Durgin?

A. Rory Calhoun.

Q. Chuck Barris wrote what Freddy Cannon hit about a southern California amusement park?

A. "Palisades Park."

———◆———

Q. Liza Minnelli received an Oscar for her role in what 1972 movie?

A. *Cabaret.*

———◆———

Q. In what year did Disneyland open in Anaheim?

A. 1955.

———◆———

Q. In 1988 Ridgecrest served as a ten-day shooting base for what science fiction movie?

A. *Star Trek V.*

———◆———

Q. In what year did Hollywood-born Stefanie Powers make her screen debut?

A. 1961.

———◆———

Q. What character did Los Angeles native Richard Boone play on the TV series "Have Gun Will Travel"?

A. Paladin.

———◆———

Q. Where was actor Robert Duvall born?

A. San Diego.

Q. On what label did Canned Heat cut its first album in 1967?

A. Liberty.

———◆———

Q. What single became a No. 1 hit for Jan and Dean in 1963?

A. "Surf City."

———◆———

Q. How many episodes of the long-running comedy series, "The Burns and Allen Show," were not done in Hollywood?

A. Only the first six.

———◆———

Q. What did the title "CHIPs" stand for in the 1977-83 TV series?

A. California Highway Patrol.

———◆———

Q. Rick's Place was a Sunset Beach hang-out in what short-lived 1979 TV series?

A. "California Fever."

———◆———

Q. What California city is home to The Walt Disney Company?

A. Burbank.

———◆———

Q. What Santa Ana actor appeared in *Flight Command, Billy the Kid, Ziegfeld Girl,* and *The Pajama Game?*

A. John Raitt.

Q. In what early 1950s situation comedy was Richard Crenna a regular?

A. "Our Miss Brooks."

———◆———

Q. Desi Arnaz, Jr., became a teenage idol as a singer/musician in what rock group?

A. Dino, Desi, and Billy.

———◆———

Q. What 1974-78 sit-com was set in the barrio of East Los Angeles?

A. "Chico and the Man."

———◆———

Q. On what Los Angeles radio station did Steve Allen host a late-night show in 1948?

A. KNX.

———◆———

Q. Born in Glendale on January 15, 1941, what is Captain Beefheart's actual name?

A. Don Van Vliet.

———◆———

Q. What facility has produced more motion pictures than any other single location in the world?

A. Burbank Studios.

———◆———

Q. In what year did Bugs Bunny come to network TV with his own show?

A. 1960.

Q. Guests on "The Tonight Show" consider it good luck to have their shoes polished by whom before going on air?

A. Floyd Jackson of Floyd's Place at NBC.

Q. What TV series about three roommates, a boy and two girls, was the third top-rated show, 1977-78?

A. "Three's Company."

Q. What Santa Barbara native co-starred with Jeff Bridges, Cybill Shepherd, and Ben Johnson in *The Last Picture Show?*

A. Timothy Bottoms.

Q. Where was session guitarist Larry Carlton born?

A. Torrance (March 2, 1948).

Q. In what 1927 Warner Brothers "talkie" did Al Jolson star?

A. *The Jazz Singer.*

Q. What firm was the first to construct a movie studio in Hollywood?

A. Nestor Film Company (1911).

Q. Who opened the pioneer Keystone Studio in Glendale?

A. Mack Sennett.

Q. Santa Monica native Robert Redford received an Oscar for directing what movie?

A. *Ordinary People.*

◆

Q. What 1964 single went No. 1 for The Beach Boys?

A. "I Get Around."

◆

Q. By what name were the Righteous Brothers first known?

A. The Paramounts.

◆

Q. David Carradine portrayed Kwai Chang Caine in what ABC Western?

A. "Kung Fu."

◆

Q. In what 1983 movie did Robert Duvall play country singer Mac Sledge?

A. *Tender Mercies.*

◆

Q. Jameson Parker and Gerald McRaney played San Diego private eyes in what TV series?

A. "Simon and Simon."

◆

Q. What southern Californian hosted the TV series "That's Incredible" with John Davidson and Fran Tarkenton?

A. Cathy Lee Crosby.

Q. What Downey duo had the 1970 No. 1 hit single "(They Long to Be) Close to You"?

A. The Carpenters.

Q. Cliff Robertson, who won an Oscar for his 1968 role in *Charley,* was born in what southern California community?

A. La Jolla (1925).

Q. Los Angeles-born actor Victor Brandt portrayed Danny Donato in what TV soap series created in 1982?

A. "Capitol."

Q. Julie Kavner received an Emmy in 1978 for her supporting role in what TV series?

A. "Rhoda."

Q. Who recorded the single "Country Boy (You Got Your Feet in L.A.)" in 1976?

A. Glen Campbell.

Q. In the early 1950s, Tennessee Ernie Ford hosted what local TV show in Los Angeles?

A. "Hometown Jamboree."

Q. Bart Braverman portrayed inept assistant Binzer in what hour-long crime show starring Robert Urich?

A. "Vegas."

Q. What actor/composer penned the scores to such movies as *Paddy, The Candidate, Jeremiah Johnson,* and *Kid Blue?*

A. John Rubinstein.

———————◆———————

Q. For what 1977 movie did Diane Keaton receive an Oscar for Best Actress?

A. *Annie Hall.*

———————◆———————

Q. Mia Farrow starred with Robert Redford in what movie about wealth in the 1920s?

A. *The Great Gatsby.*

———————◆———————

Q. What dual single went to No. 2 for Richie Valens in 1958?

A. "Donna"/"La Bamba."

———————◆———————

Q. What southern California women's quartet became famous on "The Lawrence Welk Show"?

A. The Lennon Sisters.

———————◆———————

Q. What actress won a 1981 Emmy playing Captain Doreen Lewis in the TV show "Private Benjamin"?

A. Eileen Brennan.

———————◆———————

Q. Jill St. John was on what radio series?

A. "One Man's Family."

Q. The Netherlands-born Van Halen brothers formed what group after moving to Pasadena with their family?

A. Mammoth.

---◆---

Q. In 1982 what single became No. 2 for the Go Gos?

A. "We Got the Beat."

---◆---

Q. What former U.S. Army trumpeter created one of the world's largest independent record enterprises?

A. Herb Alpert.

---◆---

Q. What Los Angeles-born actor portrayed Joe Hardy in "The Hardy Boys Mysteries" on ABC?

A. Shaun Cassidy.

---◆---

Q. What Long Beach actress appeared in such movies as *M*A*S*H*, *Brewster McCloud*, *Lost Horizon*, and *Slither?*

A. Sally Kellerman.

---◆---

Q. In what year were NBC's west coast operations first based in Burbank?

A. 1952.

---◆---

Q. Where did singer Gene Vincent of "Be-Bop-A-Lula" fame die in 1971?

A. Hollywood.

Q. What Hollywood-born actor played the husband of Norma Rae in the 1979 movie of the same name?

A. Beau Bridges.

———◆———

Q. What character did James MacArthur play in the TV series "Hawaii Five-O"?

A. Danny ("Dano") Williams.

———◆———

Q. Who are the parents of Lorenzo Lamas?

A. Arlene Dahl and Fernando Lamas.

———◆———

Q. What Pomona native composer, singer, and pianist appeared in the movies *Rumble Fish* and *Cotton Club?*

A. Tom Waits.

———◆———

Q. The Burbank Studios are presently home to what two motion picture giants?

A. Columbia Pictures and Warner Brothers.

———◆———

Q. Shelley Fabares played the teenage daughter Mary in what 1958-63 TV sit-com?

A. "The Donna Reed Show."

———◆———

Q. Richard Crenna starred with Steve McQueen in what 1966 movie set on the Yangtze River?

A. *The Sand Pebbles.*

Q. In what 1984 movie did southern Californian Jeff Bridges play an alien?

A. *Starman.*

———◆———

Q. With what singing group did Vicki Lawrence appear for three years?

A. Young Americans.

———◆———

Q. Where was Gene Walker (Gary Leeds) of The Walker Brothers born in 1944?

A. Glendale.

———◆———

Q. Where did Lou Adler discover the improvisational comedy team of Cheech and Chong?

A. Hollywood's Troubadour Club.

———◆———

Q. In 1988 Blythe became the host of what annual music celebration?

A. County Music Festival.

———◆———

Q. Portions of what 1953 movie starring William Holden as an American P.O.W. in a German prison camp were shot at Calabasas Creek?

A. *Stalag 17.*

———◆———

Q. Southern California natives Ron and Russell Mael formed what rock group in 1974?

A. Sparks.

Q. What 1983 miniseries, the second highest rated ever, starred Richard Chamberlain as a Roman Catholic priest?

A. "The Thorn Birds."

———◆———

Q. What San Diego native won Emmys in 1955 and 1956 for comedienne of the year?

A. Nanette Fabray.

———◆———

Q. What was the only major chart success for Buffalo Springfield?

A. "For What It's Worth."

———◆———

Q. What San Diego native teamed up with Stevie Nicks to record the 1974 hit single, "Gold"?

A. John Stewart.

———◆———

Q. Where was Carrie Fisher, daughter of Debbie Reynolds and Eddie Fisher, born in 1956?

A. Beverly Hills.

———◆———

Q. In what 1982 comedy film did Jeff Bridges play the role of a stuffy Egyptologist?

A. *Kiss Me Goodbye.*

———◆———

Q. Los Angeles native Mary Crosby played what role on the prime-time TV series "Dallas"?

A. Kristin (Sue Ellen's younger sister).

Q. Susan Saint James received an Emmy in 1969 for her supporting role in what TV show?

A. "The Name of the Game."

———◆———

Q. What musical group supposedly received its name from an Eskimo expression of extreme cold?

A. Three Dog Night.

———◆———

Q. Such movies as *How Green Was My Valley, Planet of the Apes,* and *The Sand Pebbles* were shot in the vicinity of what state park?

A. Malibu Creek State Park.

———◆———

Q. An Orange County canyon, island, and peak bear the last name of what nineteenth century actress?

A. Helena Modjeska.

———◆———

Q. What is Rhonda Fleming's actual name?

A. Marilyn Lewis.

———◆———

Q. In 1982 Hollywood native Morgan Brittany began playing Katherine Wentworth on what successful TV series?

A. "Dallas."

———◆———

Q. Where in San Bernardino County is the Huck Finn Country & Bluegrass Jubilee held?

A. Mojave Narrows Regional Park.

Q. Beverly Hills native Richard Chamberlain portrayed an intern at Blair General in what 1960s NBC series?

A. "Dr. Kildare."

———✦———

Q. In the TV sit-com "Dobie Gillis," what character was played by veteran Los Angeles actor William Schallert?

A. Mr. Pomfret, the English teacher.

———✦———

Q. Southern Californian Shelley Fabares recorded what hit song in the early 1960s?

A. "Johnny Angel."

———✦———

Q. What Los Angeles-born singer/songwriter has won numerous soul gospel Grammy awards?

A. Andrae Crouch.

———✦———

Q. At what age did Jodie Foster make her first TV commercial?

A. Three.

———✦———

Q. Where was actress Geraldine Chaplin born?

A. Santa Monica.

———✦———

Q. What Los Angeles public building became recognizable to millions of TV viewers on the "Dragnet" series?

A. Los Angeles City Hall.

Q. What character was played by Roger Smith in the hit TV series "77 Sunset Strip"?

A. Private eye Jeff Spencer.

——————◆——————

Q. Where was actress Sally Field born?

A. Pasadena.

——————◆——————

Q. What Beverly Hills native received a 1957 Tony for his supporting role in the Broadway play, "Bells Are Ringing"?

A. Sydney Chaplin.

——————◆——————

Q. What extravagant Los Angeles movie theater opened in 1917?

A. Million Dollar Theater.

——————◆——————

Q. Where was "One Day at a Time" actress Bonnie Franklin born?

A. Santa Monica.

——————◆——————

Q. What Los Angeles native portrayed the motorcycle riding Dr. Steven Kiley on ABC's "Marcus Welby, M.D."?

A. James Brolin.

——————◆——————

Q. Robert Stack won an Emmy in 1960 for his role in what series?

A. "The Untouchables."

Q. In what year did Leon Russell move to Los Angeles to work as a session musician?

A. 1958.

———◆———

Q. What film and television actress from Hollywood was born Suzanne Cupito?

A. Morgan Brittany.

———◆———

Q. In what extravagant brassy 1969 movie musical did the USC Trojan Marching Band appear?

A. *Hello, Dolly.*

———◆———

Q. Who developed the TV puppet series "Time for Beany"?

A. Stan Freberg.

———◆———

Q. Cher played Rusty Dennis, mother of a handicapped teenager, in what 1985 film?

A. *Mask.*

———◆———

Q. What name was given to a group of Los Angeles session singers and musicians who released the album "Uptown Festival" in 1978?

A. Shalamar.

———◆———

Q. What Los Angeles child actor starred in the 1948 movie, *The Boy with Green Hair?*

A. Dean Stockwell.

Q. What Los Angeles native was nominated for an Academy Award for best supporting actress in the 1977 film *The Goodbye Girl?*

A. Quinn Cummings.

------◆------

Q. What Los Angeles-born actress appeared in such movies as *Doc Savage, Rollerball,* and *The Nude Bomb?*

A. Pamela Hensley.

------◆------

Q. The life story of what golfing great was filmed at the Riviera golf course?

A. Ben Hogan.

------◆------

Q. What Los Angeles-born actor made his screen debut in the 1950 film, *Halls of Montezuma?*

A. Richard Boone.

------◆------

Q. Salvatore ("Sonny") Bono became mayor of what desert community?

A. Palm Springs.

------◆------

Q. Where was Shirley Temple born?

A. Santa Monica (1927).

------◆------

Q. Who did El Centro-born Ken Howard play in the short-lived 1973 TV series "Adam's Rib"?

A. Adam Bonner.

Q. What Los Angeles native was given an honorary Oscar in 1977 for distinguished service in film editing?

A. Margaret Booth.

Q. What Los Angeles-born actress starred in the 1978 movie *Halloween?*

A. Jamie Lee Curtis.

Q. Dustin Hoffman credits what California college with directing him toward an acting career?

A. Santa Monica College.

Q. Where was Herb Alpert born in 1935?

A. Los Angeles.

Q. What Los Angeles native played Natalie Green on the NBC TV show, "The Facts of Life"?

A. Mindy Cohn.

Q. Where was Timothy Hutton born?

A. Malibu.

Q. In what year did Los Angeles-born singer Natalie Cole win a Grammy as a new artist?

A. 1975.

Q. Where was Cher born on May 20, 1946?

A. El Centro.

Q. In what 1959-62 situation comedy did Jackie Cooper play a Navy doctor stationed in San Diego?

A. "Hennesey."

Q. In 1982 San Diego native Ted Danson became what character on the NBC sit-com "Cheers"?

A. Sam ("Mayday") Malone.

Q. Los Angeles native Jack Jones received a Grammy for what 1963 recording?

A. "Wives and Lovers."

Q. Santa Barbara native Joseph Bottoms created a role in what 1979 Disney science fiction film?

A. *The Black Hole*.

Q. What Santa Monica native played Sue Ellen in the TV series, "Dallas"?

A. Linda Gray.

Q. Sam Bottoms appeared in what 1979 film starring Robert Duvall, Martin Sheen, and Marlon Brando?

A. *Apocalypse Now*.

Q. What Righteous Brothers single was No. 1 in the U.S. and England in 1965?

A. "You've Lost That Loving Feeling."

———◆———

Q. What "Little House on the Prairie" actress was born in Los Angeles in 1964?

A. Melissa Gilbert.

———◆———

Q. Long Beach native Kami Cotler played what part in the long-running TV series "The Waltons"?

A. Elizabeth.

———◆———

Q. John Wayne starred with what Hollywood-born actress in the 1969 movie *True Grit?*

A. Kim Darby.

———◆———

Q. Bess Coleridge was played by what Los Angeles-born actress on the ABC soap "Ryan's Hope"?

A. Gloria DeHaven.

———◆———

Q. What former USC football star joined Don Meredith and Howard Cosell as commentator on "NFL Monday Night Football"?

A. Frank Gifford.

———◆———

Q. What Hollywood-born actress played the part of Kim Carter in the TV series, "Here's Lucy"?

A. Lucie Arnaz.

HISTORY

CHAPTER THREE

Q. How many hangings were there in Los Angeles between 1850 and 1870?

A. 77 (40 legal and 37 impromptu).

———◆———

Q. In the mid-1860s what military post protected travelers on the San Bernardino–Fort Mojave trail?

A. Camp Cady.

———◆———

Q. In what year did Richard Nixon graduate from Whittier College?

A. 1934.

———◆———

Q. Who discovered Santa Catalina Island in 1542?

A. Juan Rodriguez Cabrillo.

———◆———

Q. When Padre Garces visited the lower end of the San Joaquin Valley in 1772, what Indian tribe did he encounter?

A. Yokuts.

Q. What young topographer served with the Fremont expedition of the mid-1840s?

A. Edward Meyer Kern.

———◆———

Q. What was the population of Bakersfield in April 1869?

A. Approximately 600.

———◆———

Q. When incorporated as a city in 1911, what was the population of Burbank?

A. 3,048.

———◆———

Q. On July 25, 1797, what became the sixteenth Spanish mission founded in California?

A. Mission San Miguel Arcangel.

———◆———

Q. To whom in 1784 did the Spanish crown grant over 75,000 acres that became Rancho San Pedro?

A. Juan Jose Dominguez.

———◆———

Q. What price per acre did Griffith Dickenson and William Henry Morton pay for the 4,660-acre parcel that later became Compton?

A. 37 cents.

———◆———

Q. To meet the growing demand for water in southwestern San Diego County, construction began on what dam in 1886?

A. Sweetwater Dam.

Q. In 1909 who became the first mayor of Huntington Beach?

A. Ed Manning.

———◆———

Q. Citizens of Huntington Beach named their city after Henry Huntington because he brought what service to the community?

A. Pacific Electric Railroad.

———◆———

Q. Who established Mision San Luis Obispo de Tolosa on September 1, 1772?

A. Fra Junipero Serra.

———◆———

Q. What hostelry was constructed in Bakersfield in 1872 at a cost of $20,000?

A. Beale Hotel.

———◆———

Q. In what year was Compton Community College established as a department of Compton Union High School?

A. 1927.

———◆———

Q. What canal to bring water from the Colorado River to the Imperial Valley was completed in 1940?

A. All-American Canal.

———◆———

Q. In 1888, who became the first mayor of Compton?

A. Rudolph Sherer.

Q. How tall were the rear wheels of the Twenty Mule Team borax wagons?

A. Seven feet.

———◆———

Q. Who is recognized as Garden Grove's founding father?

A. Dr. Alonzo Cook.

———◆———

Q. The National Municipal League presented its All-American City award to what southern California community in 1980?

A. Gardena.

———◆———

Q. What scenic conveyance was opened at Palm Springs in September 1963?

A. Palm Springs Aerial Tramway.

———◆———

Q. Who in 1898 became the first white child born in the lower Coachella Valley?

A. Cinderella Courtney.

———◆———

Q. What famous general took up residence in Indio to train his troops during World War II?

A. George Patton.

———◆———

Q. Who was known as the "king of the mustang runners"?

A. Chico Martinez.

Q. Who established the socialist Kaweah Co-operative Colony in Tulare County in 1886 to cut and market lumber?

A. Burnette Haskell.

------◆------

Q. In 1911 what sugar refining firm opened a processing facility in Huntington Beach?

A. Holly Sugar Company.

------◆------

Q. Who led the Mormon Battalion to San Diego in 1847?

A. Phillip St. George Cooke.

------◆------

Q. What Whittier High School teacher did Richard Nixon marry on June 21, 1940?

A. Thelma Catherine ("Pat") Ryan.

------◆------

Q. Who in 1890 became the operator of the first resort facility in what is present-day Angeles National Forest?

A. R. W. Dawson.

------◆------

Q. In 1859 who was the first settler in the area of Kings County that later became Lemoore?

A. John Kurtz.

------◆------

Q. For whom was Fort MacArthur named in 1914?

A. Gen. Arthur MacArthur (father of Gen. Douglas MacArthur).

Q. In what year did the dependable twin-engine Douglas DC-3 go into service?

A. 1936.

———————◆———————

Q. First flown in 1924 and called the "queen of the air," what was the U.S. Navy's most successful rigid airship?

A. *Los Angeles.*

———————◆———————

Q. Until 1957, with the exception of City Hall, Los Angeles building codes limited buildings to what height?

A. 150 feet.

———————◆———————

Q. In 1949 what roads comprised the nation's first four-level interchange?

A. Harbor, Hollywood, Pasadena, and Santa Ana freeways.

———————◆———————

Q. Whose discovery of gold in about 1853 led to the Kern River gold rush?

A. Richard Keyes.

———————◆———————

Q. Later elected as state senator, James McCoy served San Diego County in what capacity from 1861 to 1871?

A. Sheriff.

———————◆———————

Q. What town served as the terminus for the twenty-mule teams from Death Valley until 1889?

A. Mojave.

Q. What project begun in 1935 is recognized as the "largest and most complete historic restoration in the West"?

A. La Purisima Mission.

―――――◆―――――

Q. In the late 1800s what transplanted New Englander became known as the "Master of Malibu"?

A. Frederick Rindge.

―――――◆―――――

Q. Where was the first oil refinery in California built in 1876?

A. Railroad Canyon.

―――――◆―――――

Q. In 1857 Fort Tejon became the western terminus of what unusual Army division?

A. The Camel Patrol.

―――――◆―――――

Q. During the 1920s, what was the most valuable single real estate holding in California?

A. Rancho Malibu.

―――――◆―――――

Q. By what name was the Pacific Coast Highway known when it was opened to traffic in June 1929?

A. Roosevelt Highway.

―――――◆―――――

Q. "Tent City" and "Gospel Swamp" were nicknames applied to Huntington Beach property donated to what religious group in 1906?

A. Methodists.

Q. Officially dedicated in 1962, what is the longest man-made small craft harbor in the world?

A. Marina del Rey.

---◆---

Q. At a cost of $900 per wagon, who designed and built the famous Twenty Mule Team borax wagons of the 1880s?

A. J. W. Perry.

---◆---

Q. In 1986 what Mojave aviator, along with Jeana Yeager, made the first non-stop, non-refueled, around-the-world flight?

A. Dick Rutan.

---◆---

Q. After a mob burned Whittier's only saloon in 1887, how long was it before another was opened in the community?

A. 53 years.

---◆---

Q. In 1918 what military base was opened in Moreno Valley to train pilots?

A. March Field (now March Air Force Base).

---◆---

Q. At what Pasadena educational and research facility did Albert Einstein work after fleeing Nazi Germany?

A. California Institute of Technology.

---◆---

Q. Who were the original inhabitants of the Santa Clarita Valley?

A. Alliklik Indians.

Q. Where in 1842 did gold flakes clinging to the roots of a wild onion set off California's first gold rush?

A. Placerita Canyon.

———◆———

Q. On January 24, 1794, what English explorer named Point Dume in honor of his friend Father Francisco Dumetz of Ventura?

A. George Vancouvere.

———◆———

Q. Henry Needham established what type of colony in the Newhall area in 1889?

A. Non-alcoholic.

———◆———

Q. What railroad tunnel constructed by Chinese laborers was the third longest in the world when completed in 1876?

A. San Fernando Railroad Tunnel.

———◆———

Q. What shepherd is credited with discovering the first California gold strike in March 1842?

A. Francisco Lopez.

———◆———

Q. The Trussel Winchester Adobe, built at Santa Barbara in 1854, utilized timbers from what wrecked ship?

A. *Winfield Scott.*

———◆———

Q. What is the second oldest school district in Los Angeles County?

A. Sulphur Springs School District.

Q. Where did Charles Crocker drive the golden spike on September 5, 1876, that completed the first railroad between Los Angeles and San Francisco?

A. Lang Station.

———◆———

Q. What notorious Mexican bandit was hanged on March 18, 1875?

A. Tiburcio Vasquez.

———◆———

Q. Where in 1928 was the last great train robbery staged in California?

A. Saugus.

———◆———

Q. In the March 12, 1928, collapse of the Francisquito Canyon Dam, how much water was released?

A. 12 billion gallons (causing some 450 deaths).

———◆———

Q. In 1838 who was granted 75 square miles of southern California land that he named Rancho San Francisco?

A. Antonio del Valle.

———◆———

Q. What Indian village formerly occupied the site of present-day Castaic Junction?

A. Chaguayabit.

———◆———

Q. What military post was established August 10, 1854, to stop cattle rustlers and protect local Indians?

A. Fort Tejon.

Q. In 1949 what firm began the tenth largest suburban real estate development in the nation?

A. Lakewood Park Corporation.

———◆———

Q. In 1904 Frederick Rindge constructed what 20-mile southern California railroad?

A. Hueneme, Malibu, and Port Los Angeles Railway.

———◆———

Q. What historic hotel was erected at Lancaster in 1876?

A. Western Hotel.

———◆———

Q. Who founded a utopian socialist colony in Antelope Valley in 1914?

A. Job Harriman.

———◆———

Q. What community college opened in Huntington Beach in 1966?

A. Golden West College.

———◆———

Q. What house served as the center of social life in the San Fernando Valley during the late 1800s?

A. La Casa de Geronimo Lopez.

———◆———

Q. What was the first evidence of European industry in the Los Angeles area?

A. The Chatsworth Lime Kiln.

Q. With parts of the structure dating back to 1834, what is the oldest house in the San Fernando Valley?

A. Andres Pico Adobe.

◆

Q. In 1865 retired Los Angeles sheriff Thomas Sanchez built the Casa Adobe de San Rafael as a home for his wife and how many children?

A. 19.

◆

Q. The Mexican War in California ended with the signing of what treaty on January 13, 1847?

A. Treaty of Cahuenga.

◆

Q. When incorporated in 1903, Hollywood had how many male residents?

A. 177.

◆

Q. What attorney, rancher, and Civil War hero is credited with starting in 1887 the settlement that became Gardena?

A. Spencer Roane Thorpe.

◆

Q. Founded in 1769, what is the largest of the California missions?

A. San Luis Rey.

◆

Q. The Balboa Pavilion was opened in 1905 to coincide with the completion of what public service to the area?

A. The Pacific Electric Red Car Line.

Q. For what amount did the first lot on Balboa Island in Newport Bay sell in 1908?

A. $700.

Q. In the late 1890s, who became Palm Springs' first hotel proprietor?

A. Dr. Welwood Murry.

Q. The town site for Oceanside was laid-out by what surveyor for Andrew Jackson Myers in 1883?

A. Cave J. Couts, Jr.

Q. In what year was Camp Joseph H. Pendleton established?

A. 1942.

Q. Who designed and began manufacturing electric irons at Ontario in 1902?

A. E. H. Richardson.

Q. Built in 1884, what is the oldest remaining building in Palm Springs?

A. The McCallum Adobe.

Q. What Newhall resident ran for U.S. Senator on the Prohibition ticket and was a favorite-son candidate for U.S. president in 1920?

A. Henry Clay Needham.

Q. By what name was Mission Inn first called in 1876?

A. Glenwood Cottages.

---◆---

Q. In 1851 who led some 500 immigrants from Salt Lake City to establish the Mormon settlement of San Bernardino?

A. Captain Jefferson Hunt.

---◆---

Q. Founded in 1786, what California mission is known as the "Queen of the Missions"?

A. Santa Barbara.

---◆---

Q. Built at Santa Monica, what was the name of the 1924 Douglas World Cruiser, the first airplane to fly around the world?

A. *New Orleans.*

---◆---

Q. Who built the first Danish-style windmill at Solvang in 1947?

A. Ferdinand Sorensen.

---◆---

Q. In 1863 what former Texas Ranger became the first white man to build a home in Spring Valley?

A. August Ensworth.

---◆---

Q. In 1910 the Interstate Realty and Improvement Company offered a lot in their East San Diego Villa Heights subdivision with the purchase of what item?

A. A $109 set of encyclopedias.

Q. What Pasadena businessman started the development of Torrance as an industrial site in 1913?

A. Jared Torrance.

Q. In 1902 blacksmith Al Bowe and jeweler H. H. Hooper became the first persons to manufacture what product in Whittier?

A. Automobiles.

Q. In 1904 what firm established permanent telephone service to 80 homes in Whittier?

A. Home Telephone Company.

Q. In what year did T. L. Tally open his Phonograph and Vitascope Parlor in Los Angeles?

A. 1896.

Q. In a 1903 ordinance, it became a misdemeanor to drive more than how many sheep through Hollywood in one herd?

A. 2,000.

Q. In 1880 Methodists founded what southern California school in a mustard field?

A. University of Southern California.

Q. What event set an attendance record of 134,254 at the Los Angeles Coliseum on September 8, 1963?

A. Billy Graham Crusade.

Q. What price did W. E. Willmore charge for lots in his 1881 Willmore City, a forerunner of Long Beach?

A. $12.50 to $25.

———◆———

Q. In 1938 what pilot took off from Long Beach to New York in a flight that earned him the nickname "Wrong-way" when he landed in Ireland instead on the "return" trip?

A. Douglas Corrigan.

———◆———

Q. By what title was Pasadena's Orange Grove Avenue known during the 1890s?

A. "Millionaires' Row."

———◆———

Q. In what year was Mount Wilson Observatory founded?

A. 1904.

———◆———

Q. What school was the forerunner of the California Institute of Technology?

A. Throop University.

———◆———

Q. What is the oldest Spanish settlement in California?

A. San Diego.

———◆———

Q. For what was Father Marcos and his followers searching when they visited the site of present-day San Diego in 1539?

A. The "Seven Cities of Cibola."

Q. What English scientific research sloop visited San Diego in 1793?

A. *Discovery.*

---◆---

Q. What was the *Lelia Byrd* smuggling when it engaged the battery at Ballet Point in a cannon duel?

A. Otter skins.

---◆---

Q. In the mid-1800s who was the first person to build a house in the "New Town" area of San Diego?

A. William Heath Davis.

---◆---

Q. In 1940 what was the only large-scale industrial plant in San Diego?

A. Consolidated Aircraft.

---◆---

Q. What railroad company laid tracks into San Diego in 1885?

A. Santa Fe Railroad.

---◆---

Q. In what southern California city was Charles A. Lindbergh's *Spirit of St. Louis* manufactured?

A. San Diego.

---◆---

Q. From approximately 40,000 residents in 1887, to what populaton did San Diego decline by 1890?

A. 17,000.

Q. On June 21, 1913, at Los Angeles, who became the first woman to parachute from an airplane?

A. Georgia Broadwick.

———◆———

Q. In what year did the last survivor of the Canalino Indian tribe of the Channel Islands die?

A. 1930.

———◆———

Q. The severe drought of 1864 caused the cattle population in Santa Barbara County to drop from 200,000 to what figure?

A. 5,000.

———◆———

Q. To whom was Ronald Reagan married from 1940 to 1948?

A. Actress Jane Wyman.

———◆———

Q. Sale deeds in California's first successful land colonization project in 1874 prohibited the sale of what product?

A. Liquor.

———◆———

Q. Through what Santa Lucia Mountains pass did John Fremont lead his army to capture San Luis Obispo in November 1846?

A. Cuesta Pass.

———◆———

Q. What California mission begun in 1797 and completed in 1806 was named in honor of a Crusader?

A. Mission San Juan Capistrano.

Q. Who established the headquarters of his Rosicrucian Fellowship at Oceanside in 1911?

A. Max Heindel.

Q. On what date did California formally become a territory of the Mexican Republic?

A. March 26, 1825.

Q. On January 15, 1816, who disembarked from the *Albatross* near Santa Barbara to become California's first American settler?

A. Thomas Doak.

Q. How many Mexican colonists from San Blas arrived at San Diego on September 1, 1834?

A. 200.

Q. On January 19, 1847, who was appointed as the first American Governor of California?

A. John C. Fremont.

Q. When did President Millard Fillmore sign the act admitting California into the Union as a state?

A. September 9, 1850.

Q. What means of public transportation first reached San Diego from San Antonio on August 31, 1857?

A. Overland stage.

Q. What two labor leaders were convicted in the October 1, 1910, dynamiting of the Los Angeles *Times* building?

A. James B. and John J. McNamara.

———◆———

Q. The May 19, 1913, California Land Act prohibited what ethnic group from owning agricultural land in California?

A. Japanese.

———◆———

Q. Where was the 1915 Panama-California Exposition held?

A. San Diego.

———◆———

Q. During the 1970s, how much southern California land was urbanized every day?

A. 250 acres.

———◆———

Q. A $500 fine was levied against Santa Barbara in 1848 by Governor Mason to encourage the settlement to give up what item?

A. A 12-pound brass cannon.

———◆———

Q. What two radio stations opened in Los Angeles in 1922?

A. KFI and KHJ.

———◆———

Q. In 1910 an 11,000-foot breakwater was constructed to better protect what harbor from the Pacific Ocean?

A. San Pedro.

Q. What Progressive political organization was called the Goo-Goos by their enemies?

A. The Good Government Group.

———◆———

Q. During the 1960s, what Mexican-American organized migrant farm workers and created the United Farm Workers of America?

A. Cesar Chavez.

———◆———

Q. Who was arrested at San Pedro during the 1923 seaman's strike while reading the Declaration of Independence?

A. Upton Sinclair.

———◆———

Q. In 1865 who became the first banker in southern California?

A. I. W. Hellman.

———◆———

Q. At what location in Los Angeles was oil first discovered in 1893 by digging with a pick and shovel?

A. Corner of West State Street and Patton.

———◆———

Q. On December 31, 1892, what city became the first in southern California to receive commercial hydroelectric power?

A. Pomona.

———◆———

Q. What type of air mail and express service was inaugurated in Los Angeles on October 1, 1947?

A. Helicopter.

Q. What American aviator established an altitude record at Los Angeles on January 12, 1910?

A. Louis Paulhan.

———◆———

Q. In what year were naval orange trees first brought to Riverside from Brazil?

A. 1873.

———◆———

Q. What colorful female evangelist and founder of the Church of the Four-square Gospel constructed the 5,000-seat Angelus Temple in Los Angeles in 1923?

A. Aimee Semple McPherson.

———◆———

Q. What correctional facility was opened in Cummings Valley in 1932?

A. California Institute for Women.

———◆———

Q. Who blazed the Spanish Trail through Cajon Pass from Santa Fe to Los Angeles in 1831?

A. William Wolfskill.

———◆———

Q. Who planted Glendora's first commercial orange grove in 1866?

A. John Cook.

———◆———

Q. What was the construction cost of the Colorado River Aqueduct?

A. $220 million.

HISTORY

Q. National attention was focused on the Imperial Valley in 1934 when what type of laborers went on strike?

A. Lettuce pickers (8,000 strong).

———◆———

Q. Who served as sheriff of Los Angeles county from 1932 to 1958?

A. Eugene Biscailuz.

———◆———

Q. Because of his monopoly on landing facilities at San Pedro harbor, during the 1850s and 60s Phineas Banning was given what title?

A. "The Port Admiral."

———◆———

Q. In 1973 what incumbent did Tom Bradley defeat to become the first black mayor of Los Angeles?

A. Sam Yorty.

———◆———

Q. What noted racketeer grew up in the East Los Angeles area of Boyle Heights?

A. Meyer ("Mickey") Cohen.

———◆———

Q. Who became Hollywood's first make-up artist when he opened a shop in downtown Los Angeles in 1909?

A. Max Factor.

———◆———

Q. In the late 1930s, what gaming ship anchored in Santa Monica Bay generated $100,000 a month for the Capone mob?

A. *Rex.*

Q. What Depression-era police chief invented the "bum blockade" to discourage indigents from moving to Los Angeles?

A. James Davis.

———◆———

Q. What mansion, complete with 22 bathrooms and a shooting gallery, did automobile manufacturer Errett Cord build in Beverly Hills?

A. Cordhaven.

———◆———

Q. On its maiden, and only, flight, Howard Hughes' "Spruce Goose" flew what distance?

A. One mile.

———◆———

Q. Prior to 1919, what was the spelling of Lockheed Aircraft at Santa Barbara?

A. Loughead.

———◆———

Q. At the height of the Vietnam War, what portion of the San Diego work force was military related?

A. 70 percent.

———◆———

Q. Unemployment in Los Angeles County was at what level by mid-1934, during the height of the Depression?

A. 300,000.

———◆———

Q. How many Japanese-Americans in California were removed to internment centers during World War II?

A. Approximately 110,000.

ARTS & LITERATURE

C H A P T E R   F O U R

Q. What Long Beach-born syndicated columnist won a Pulitzer prize in 1972 for national reporting?

A. Jack Anderson.

Q. Who designed the Riverside Art Museum building?

A. Julia Morgan (1929).

Q. Where is the Kern Shakespeare Festival held each summer?

A. Bakersfield.

Q. How many seats are there in the Hollywood Bowl?

A. 17,619.

Q. What prolific writer and naturalist organized the Sierra Club?

A. John Muir.

Q. Published in 1950, what was Ray Bradbury's first book?

A. *Martian Chronicles.*

———◆———

Q. The J. Paul Getty Museum is modeled after what first century Herculaneum country house?

A. Villa dei Papiri.

———◆———

Q. What was the most noted work that Thomas Mann produced while living in southern California, 1941-52?

A. *Dr. Faustus.*

———◆———

Q. What community is the home of the High Desert Symphony Association?

A. Victorville.

———◆———

Q. Attracting artists from across the Southwest, what spring art show is sponsored by the Hesperia Parks and Recreation District?

A. Old Town Art Show.

———◆———

Q. What British novelist dabbled in spiritualism while at Phelan?

A. Aldous Huxley.

———◆———

Q. Who merged the *Daily Times* and the *Weekly Mirror* in 1882 to form the Los Angeles *Times?*

A. Col. (later Gen.) Harrison Gray Otis.

Q. What Santa Barbara resident who began writing children's books after her father died wrote *Rebecca of Sunnybrook Farm?*

A. Kate Douglas Wiggin.

Q. In 1946 what organization was founded in Bakersfield to promote and support church and sacred music?

A. American Guild of Organists.

Q. What Calahasas woodcarver became known nationally for his miniature cowboys and horses?

A. Andy Anderson.

Q. What Carlsbad summer celebration features a series of symphony "Pops" concerts?

A. Batiquitos Festival.

Q. The Catalina Casino, one of the world's best examples of art deco architecture, was built in what year?

A. 1929.

Q. What early southern California author's works were sympathetic toward the oft-maligned sheepherders?

A. Mary Austin.

Q. What Watts-born poet and writer became the first black to receive an Emmy for daytime television?

A. Wanda Coleman.

Q. In what year did the black newspaper, *California Eagle*, first go to press in Los Angeles?

A. 1879.

Q. *Ascension* (1976) and *Liberator of the Spirit* (1982) are both collections of poetry by what Compton resident?

A. Kamau Daa'ood.

Q. What contemporary Los Angeles-born sculptor is known for his revolutionary Hispuf art style in plastics?

A. Charles Dickson.

Q. What is the name of the newspaper published in Fallbrook?

A. *The Enterprise.*

Q. What gifted California poet took his pseudonym from one of his heroes, bandit Joaquin Murietta?

A. Joaquin Miller.

Q. Measuring 45 feet in height and 195 feet in length, where may the world's largest religious painting be viewed?

A. Forest Lawn, Glendale.

Q. College of the Desert is home to what internationally known music contest?

A. Joanna Hodges Piano Competition.

Q. What facility that opened in January 1988 is Phase One of the Bob Hope Cultural Center?

A. McCallum Theatre for the Performing Arts.

———◆———

Q. What feature writer for the New York *Sun* wrote stories of borax mining and the 20-mule teams of Death Valley?

A. John Spears.

———◆———

Q. What Bakersfield choral group is known for its annual performance of Handel's *Messiah?*

A. Masterworks Chorale.

———◆———

Q. In 1912 what weekly newspaper and forerunner of the Indio *Daily News* began publication?

A. *The Date Palm.*

———◆———

Q. Where is the Oakleaf Music Festival held?

A. Conejo Community Park, Thousand Oaks.

———◆———

Q. The emergence of Los Angeles from pueblo to modern city was most thoroughly chronicled by what noted social historian?

A. Hildegarde Hawthorne.

———◆———

Q. Who created the sculpture *Young Lincoln* on display in the Los Angeles United States Court House?

A. James L. Hausers.

Q. What local newspaper services the La Habra area?

A. *Daily Star-Progress.*

———◆———

Q. Helen Hunt Jackson used what rancho for the setting of her 1884 novel, *Ramona?*

A. Camulos.

———◆———

Q. What news reporter wrote of the gold strike of the Rand mining district?

A. Henry Tinsley.

———◆———

Q. What facility is the home of Ontario's theater-in-the-round?

A. Gallery Theater.

———◆———

Q. What 2½-acre garden walk in Palm Springs features international contemporary sculpture?

A. Aerie Sculpture Garden.

———◆———

Q. What facility in Riverside is one of the major centers in the West featuring the history, art, and technology of photography?

A. California Museum of Photography.

———◆———

Q. What experimental Frank Norris novel ended with a bitter confrontation in Death Valley?

A. *McTeague.*

Q. The Dorothy Chandler Pavilion, Mark Taper Forum, and Ahmanson Theatre collectively form what facility?

A. Los Angeles Music Center.

———◆———

Q. Who built the Lincoln Shrine in Redlands featuring a bust of Abraham Lincoln by New York sculptor George Barnard?

A. Robert Watchorns.

———◆———

Q. What journalist detailed the construction of "the ditch in the desert," the Los Angeles Aqueduct?

A. E. Roscoe Shrader.

———◆———

Q. In 1873 what Italian musician built Santa Barbara's first theater?

A. Jose Lobero.

———◆———

Q. Where was the Pacific Conservatory of the Performing Arts founded in 1964?

A. Allan Hancock College, Santa Maria.

———◆———

Q. In *Oil!* what famed novelist wrote of the disgraceful conditions following the discovery of the Signal Oil Field?

A. Upton Sinclair.

———◆———

Q. In what year was the present J. Paul Getty Museum in Malibu opened to the public?

A. 1974.

Q. Who founded the Bakersfield Mexican Folk Dance troop, Los Correcaminos?

A. Lupe de la Rosa.

———◆———

Q. What author was the self-appointed publicist of Palm Springs?

A. J. Smeaton Chase.

———◆———

Q. How many times was John Steven McGroarty's romantic pageant, *The Mission Play,* performed at San Gabriel before closing in 1933?

A. 3,300.

———◆———

Q. Whittier is named for what 1800s Pennsylvania poet, writer, and newspaper editor?

A. John Greenleaf Whittier.

———◆———

Q. Where does the Hi-Desert Playhouse Guild provide year-round productions and special cultural events?

A. Joshua Tree.

———◆———

Q. From what author of *The Daring Young Man on the Flying Trapeze* did America learn about Fresno?

A. William Saroyan.

———◆———

Q. In what year was the Twenty-nine Palms art gallery built?

A. 1936.

Q. What artists' colony was promoted by Col. Ed Fletcher and William B. Gross around 1900?

A. Grossmont.

◆

Q. What half-Cherokee author perpetrated a literary hoax with *The Life and Adventures of Joaquin Murietta?*

A. John R. Ridge ("Yellow Bird").

◆

Q. What American novelist was honored in the 1906 naming of a Los Angeles community?

A. Nathaniel Hawthorne (Hawthorne).

◆

Q. What Walter Scott novel provided a name for a Tulare County community?

A. *Ivanhoe.*

◆

Q. What Budd Schulberg novel attacks the artificiality of Hollywood?

A. *What Makes Sammy Run?*

◆

Q. What southern California landmark was the model for Evelyn Waugh's satire, *The Loved One?*

A. Forest Lawn Memorial Park.

◆

Q. What English author satirized the California way of death in *After Many a Summer Dies the Swan?*

A. Aldous Huxley.

Q. During the 1910s and 20s, what socialist newspaper rivaled the circulation of the *Los Angeles Times?*

A. *The Appeal to Reason.*

———◆———

Q. D. W. Griffith's most famous movie, *Birth of a Nation,* was based on what Thomas Dixon novel?

A. *The Clansman.*

———◆———

Q. What 1839 book detailed a scheme whereby investors holding Mexican bonds could trade them for California land?

A. *California: A History of Upper and Lower California.*

———◆———

Q. What book presented a scholarly look at the working conditions of California's migrant worker?

A. *Factories in the Fields.*

———◆———

Q. Many critics consider what Frank Norris book to be the first important novel about California?

A. *The Octopus.*

———◆———

Q. Author Harold Bell Wright named what Imperial County community in 1910?

A. Meloland.

———◆———

Q. What eight-foot stone sculpture by Archibald Garner is on display at the United States Court House in Los Angeles?

A. *Law.*

Q. What Bakersfield playwright wrote *Growing Gracefully: The Middle Ages of Women?*

A. Mary Ann Fritts.

Q. What F. Scott Fitzgerald novel about the film industry was made into a film starring Robert DeNiro?

A. *The Last Tycoon.*

Q. Who created the Triforium in Los Angeles?

A. Joseph Young.

Q. Who in 1933 painted the murals in the Los Angeles Public Library depicting the history of California?

A. Dean Cornwell.

Q. What two architects designed the Capital Cathedral?

A. Philip Johnson and John Burgee.

Q. What author created private investigator Phillip Marlowe?

A. Raymond Chandler.

Q. What Dashiell Hammet novel was filmed three times in eleven years?

A. *The Maltese Falcon.*

Q. What magazine, inspired by a famous radio show, was responsible for that show's return to the air?

A. *The Shadow.*

Q. What wilderness author was the first director of the U.S. Geological Survey?

A. Clarence King.

Q. What author turned Joseph Walker's discovery of a pass through the Sierra Mountains into a disgrace?

A. Washington Irving.

Q. What southern California landmark is named for the author of *Two Years Before the Mast?*

A. Dana Point (for Richard Dana).

Q. What social reformer wrote *A Century of Dishonor,* a report on the treatment of Spanish/Mexicans in southern California?

A. Helen Hunt Jackson.

Q. What Robert Leslie Bellem private investigator was based in Hollywood?

A. Dan Turner, Hollywood Detective.

Q. What 1938 Rita Hayworth film was taken from Cornell Woolrich's story, "Angel Face"?

A. *Convicted.*

Q. What famous fictional attorney has appeared in 82 novels, 3 short stories, 6 films, a radio series, a television series, and several television movies?

A. Perry Mason.

———◆———

Q. What southern California hero of Ross Macdonald was portrayed by Paul Newman in *Harper* and *The Drowning Pool?*

A. Lew Archer.

———◆———

Q. Although he worked for 3½ years as a scriptwriter, what was F. Scott Fitzgerald's only screen credit?

A. *Three Comrades.*

———◆———

Q. What James M. Cain novel has been filmed twice, the last starring Jack Nicholson and Jessica Lange?

A. *The Postman Always Rings Twice.*

———◆———

Q. What 1925 autobiography describes how New England and Spanish influences defined the heritage of southern California?

A. *Adobe Days,* by Bixby Smith.

———◆———

Q. What Los Angeles minister wrote *The Better City,* a program for moral and organizational renewal of the city?

A. Dana Bartlett.

———◆———

Q. What book was called the Pepys' diary of Los Angeles?

A. *Sixty Years in Southern California,* by Harris Newmark.

Q. What stage play that ran from 1912 to 1929 resulted in such honors as its author being named Poet Laureate of California?

A. *The Mission Play,* by John S. McGroarty.

———◆———

Q. The 1923-24 Mission Playhouse now serves as what civic facility?

A. San Gabriel Civic Auditorium.

———◆———

Q. Noted landscape architect, Frederick Law Olmsted, planned what California model city in 1911?

A. Torrance.

———◆———

Q. Where is the home of the California Institute of the Arts?

A. Valencia.

———◆———

Q. What prolific writer of essays, short stories, and screenplays also promoted Chevrolet's Geo in TV commercials?

A. Harlan Ellison.

———◆———

Q. What social commentator coined the phrases "Kook Phase," "Window on Tomorrow," and "Open Skull Phase" in describing California's history?

A. Art Seidenbaum.

———◆———

Q. What Los Angeles magazine became *Wilshire's Magazine* after it was moved to New York City?

A. *Challenge.*

Q. *The Trojan Heritage,* a book about USC's football history, was written in 1980 by what southern California newspaperman?

A. Mal Florence.

Q. First published on May 17, 1851, what four-page weekly, bilingual publication was Los Angeles' first newspaper?

A. *Star,* or *La Estrella de Los Angeles.*

Q. What writer's stay at a cheap Hollywood motel resulted in *The Day of the Locusts,* a satirical look at the film industry?

A. Nathanael West.

Q. Where is the Cunningham Memorial Art Gallery?

A. Bakersfield.

Q. Painted on sail-cloth by Indians, where was the *Stations of the Cross* series produced during the 1770s?

A. Mission San Gabriel.

Q. In what year was the Los Angeles Philharmonic founded?

A. 1919.

Q. What notable art gallery opened in Los Angeles in 1903?

A. Southwest Museum.

Q. What is the home of the Los Angeles Civic Light Opera and Philharmonic Orchestra?

A. The Dorothy Chandler Pavilion.

———◆———

Q. What open-air concert facility in a natural amphitheater in the Cahuenga Hills was formally dedicated in 1922?

A. The Hollywood Bowl.

———◆———

Q. What Rodin bronze sculpture dominates the reflecting pool of the Los Angeles County Museum of Art?

A. *Honore de Balzac.*

———◆———

Q. Established in May 1851, what was San Diego's first newspaper?

A. *Herald.*

———◆———

Q. The Conejo Players bring community theater to what city?

A. Thousand Oaks.

———◆———

Q. What architect designed the unique Wayfarers Chapel at Portuguese Bend?

A. Lloyd Wright (son of Frank Lloyd Wright).

———◆———

Q. The Norton Simon Museum, one of the most influential new museums of art in California, is situated in what city?

A. Pasadena.

Q. A "First Folio" of William Shakespeare's plays and Ben Franklin's handwritten autobiography are in what San Marino facility?

A. Huntington Library.

———◆———

Q. What poem inspired the play and film *A Fool There Was?*

A. "The Vampire," by Rudyard Kipling.

———◆———

Q. Under what name does Newhall resident Jamie Alder publish his surrealist-style cartoons?

A. Bill Shut.

———◆———

Q. What Santa Monica illustrator and graphic designer produced the 1979 award-winning album cover design for the group Chicago?

A. Gary Meyer.

———◆———

Q. Where did painter and etcher Thomas Moran die in 1926?

A. Santa Barbara.

———◆———

Q. What Los Angeles firm designed the high-tech AT&T globe logo?

A. Saul Bass and Associates.

———◆———

Q. Where was watercolor artist Rexford Elson Brandt born in 1914?

A. San Diego.

Q. What muralist and illustrator known for his scenes of Indians and the Old West was born in Los Angeles in 1881?

A. Hernando Gonzallo Villa.

◆

Q. In 1968 who created an aluminum and bronze sculpture for the Stanley Folb Building in Hollywood?

A. Gloria Burton.

◆

Q. What support group for the fine arts was organized in Los Angeles in 1925?

A. Los Angeles Art Association.

◆

Q. Who sculpted the Will Rogers Memorial Tablet for 20th Century-Fox?

A. Roger Noble Burnham.

◆

Q. In 1982 what noted illustrator became an instructor of analytical drawing at the Art Center of Design in Pasadena?

A. Burne Hogarth.

◆

Q. Who received "Chair of Great Cartoonists" from the student body of UCLA in 1975?

A. David Berg.

◆

Q. In what year was the Los Angeles County Museum of Art founded?

A. 1961.

Q. In what community is the A. K. Smiley Public Library?

A. Redlands.

———◆———

Q. In what year was the Fine Arts Society of San Diego established?

A. 1925.

———◆———

Q. What Long Beach cartoonist created Frank the Unicorn?

A. Phil Yeh.

———◆———

Q. During the 1920s what mural painter produced the work *Romance* for the William Penn Hotel in Whittier?

A. Conrad Buff.

———◆———

Q. Animator Joe Barbera helped set up a new animation department for what studio in 1937?

A. Metro-Goldwyn-Mayer (MGM).

———◆———

Q. What southern California sculptor created the Southwest Museum's works *Pete* and *Dry Water Hole?*

A. Ella Buchanan.

———◆———

Q. Eldon Dedini, who received Best Color Cartoon award from *Playboy* in 1978, attended what Los Angeles art school, 1942-44?

A. Chouined Art Institute.

Q. What southern California painter received a gold medal for his work at the 1928 Pacific Southwest Exposition?

A. William Wendt.

———◆———

Q. What Italian-born sculptor produced works for the Los Angeles Civic Center and the Santa Barbara Court House?

A. Ettore Cadorin.

———◆———

Q. What animator who worked on early *Looney Tunes* later developed the characters of Beany and Cecil the Seasick Sea Serpent?

A. Robert ("Bob") Clampett.

———◆———

Q. What southern California Hungarian immigrant received gold medals for his paintings at the 1910 and 1916 Panama-Pacific expositions?

A. Maurice Braun.

———◆———

Q. The Zane Gray Pueblo in Avalon is now used for what purpose?

A. A hotel.

———◆———

Q. In *The Grapes of Wrath*, what highway brought John Steinbeck's displaced characters to southern California?

A. U.S. 66.

———◆———

Q. Lawyer and soldier of fortune Horace Bell was editor of what 1860s Los Angeles publication?

A. *Porcupine*.

ARTS & LITERATURE

Q. At what age did Edgar Rice Burroughs begin his writing career?

A. 35 years.

Q. What 1953 novel by Ray Bradbury was an allegorical protest against McCarthyism?

A. *Fahrenheit 451.*

Q. Who took over California's major Democratic newspaper, the *Los Angeles Daily News,* in 1926?

A. Elias Manchester Boddy.

Q. The removable sounding shell of the Hollywood Bowl was designed by what famous architect?

A. Lloyd Wright (son of Frank Lloyd Wright).

Q. Who conducted the Los Angeles Philharmonic, 1961-78?

A. Zubin Mehta.

Q. *The Postman Always Rings Twice* (1934), *Double Indemnity* (1936), and *Mildred Pierce* (1941) are the three major works of what southern California author?

A. James Maliahas Cain.

Q. As a Los Angeles high school student, Ray Bradbury founded what magazine?

A. *Future Fantasia.*

Q. What famous *Lord of the Apes* character did Edgar Rice Burroughs create?

A. Tarzan.

———◆———

Q. Simon Rodia (Sam Rodilia) spent 30 years constructing what ornate monumental piece of sculpture?

A. The *Watts Towers*.

———◆———

Q. Known during his time as Hollywood's most outrageous publicity agent, Russell Juarez Birdwell wrote what fictional memoir in 1939?

A. *I Ring Doorbells*.

———◆———

Q. In what year did writer Earle Stanley Gardner arrive in Oxnard to open a law office?

A. 1911.

———◆———

Q. What cemetery owner of Forest Lawn fame assembled the largest collection of marble statuary in the nation?

A. Hubert Eaton.

———◆———

Q. In 1941 what world renowned Russian-born composer settled in Hollywood?

A. Igor Fedorovich Stravinsky.

———◆———

Q. What Los Angeles architect designed the 1954 circular Capitol Records Tower?

A. Welton David Beckett.

Q. What southern Californian and his wife spent 22 years writing the *Story of Civilization?*

A. William James ("Will") Durant.

———◆———

Q. Arriving in Los Angeles in 1915, who established the Society of Spiritual Arts, advocating dance as a religious ritual?

A. "Miss Ruth" St. Denis (Ruth Dannis).

———◆———

Q. Under what pseudonym did Earle Stanley Gardner at times write?

A. A. A. Fair.

———◆———

Q. What well known novelist wrote the screenplay adaptation of Raymond Chandler's *The Big Sleep?*

A. William Faulkner.

———◆———

Q. What English author of *Three Weeks* was invited to Hollywood in 1920 as an authority on romantic sex?

A. Elinor Sutherland Glyn.

———◆———

Q. How many film versions of Zane Grey's *Riders of the Purple Sage* did Hollywood produce?

A. Four.

———◆———

Q. What one-time violist with the Los Angeles Symphony composed *Death Valley Suite, Hollywood Suite,* and *Grand Canyon Suite?*

A. Ferde Grofe.

Q. *The Splash* and *A Bigger Splash* are works produced by what English painter who relocated to southern California in 1963?

A. David Hockney.

Q. What was gossip columnist Hedda Hooper's actual name?

A. Elda Furry.

Q. Although known as a novelist and film critic, what author worked with John Houston on the screenplay for *The African Queen?*

A. James Agee.

Q. Edward Kienhoiz, an avant-guard Los Angeles artist of the 1950s and 60s, created what 1964 sculpture featuring mannequin lovers?

A. *Back Seat Dodge '38.*

Q. What popular novel did Helen Hunt Jackson write when her report, *A Century of Dishonor,* was ignored?

A. *Ramona.*

Q. What Hollywood writer was the author of *I Cover the Waterfront* and *Second House from the Corner?*

A. Max Miller.

Q. What New York journalist was sent to cover California's constitutional convention for the New York *Tribune?*

A. Bayard Taylor.

SPORTS & LEISURE

CHAPTER FIVE

Q. What was O.J. Simpson's original name?

A. Orenthal James Simpson.

———◆———

Q. Who was the first college coach to win bowl games in seven consecutive seasons?

A. UCLA coach Terry Donahue.

———◆———

Q. What golf course is the site of the Los Angeles Open?

A. Riviera.

———◆———

Q. Ontario-born Del Crandall spent most of his major league years with what ball club?

A. Boston and Milwaukee Braves.

———◆———

Q. In what year was Dodger Stadium opened?

A. 1962.

Q. USC football coach Howard Jones "created" what position in modern football?

A. Tailback.

———◆———

Q. What southern Californian was named AP Athlete of the Year in 1963 and 1964?

A. Mickey Wright (LPGA golfing).

———◆———

Q. How many NCAA titles did John Wooden's UCLA teams win?

A. Ten.

———◆———

Q. In April 1958, what hurler threw the first pitch for the Los Angeles Dodgers?

A. Carl Erskine.

———◆———

Q. How many world championships did the Los Angeles Lakers win in the 1980s?

A. Five.

———◆———

Q. What was John McKay's win-loss record as head coach at USC?

A. 127-40-8 (.749).

———◆———

Q. What San Diego Padre led the National League in hitting three times from 1984 to 1988?

A. Tony Gwynn.

Q. What team did USC deprive of a national championship with its 20-17 win in 1964?

A. Notre Dame.

———◆———

Q. Who was the number one selection in the 1989 NFL draft?

A. UCLA quarterback Troy Aikman.

———◆———

Q. In what year did the UCLA Bruins basketball team win their first ever National Invitational Tournament?

A. 1985.

———◆———

Q. USC running back Sam Cunningham (1970-72) attended what secondary school?

A. Santa Barbara High School.

———◆———

Q. UCLA end Burr Baldwin (1944-46) was born in what city?

A. Bakersfield.

———◆———

Q. Through the 1988 season, who ranks as UCLA's all-time leading placekicker?

A. John Lee.

———◆———

Q. Where do the Los Angeles Kings (NHL) play their home games?

A. The Forum.

Q. Golfing great Nancy Lopez was born in what California city?

A. Torrance.

———◆———

Q. What San Diego State cornerback was MVP in the 1971 East-West Shrine game after intercepting three passes?

A. Willie Buchanon.

———◆———

Q. What USC defensive back was the 1967 NCAA punt return leader with 570 yards, 47 returns?

A. Michael Battle.

———◆———

Q. What was the starting line-up for the 1972-73 UCLA basketball team?

A. Larry Farmer, Keith Wilkes, Bill Walton, Larry Hollyfield, and Greg Lee.

———◆———

Q. When formed in 1887, the Los Angeles Country Club used what objects for cups on the nine-hole course?

A. Tomato cans.

———◆———

Q. Where was football commissioner Pete Rozelle born?

A. South Gate.

———◆———

Q. What UCLA quarterbacks rank as the top three in single-season passing?

A. Troy Aikman (1988), Tom Ramsey (1982), and Rick Neuheisel (1983).

Q. What Hermosa Beach-born quarterback led the USC Trojans to a national championship in 1962?

A. Peter ("Pete") Beathard.

———◆———

Q. The passing of what Covina-born quarterback led USC to a 1931 victory over Notre Dame?

A. Gus Shavel.

———◆———

Q. Los Angeles native Bobby Doerr played for what major league club, 1937-51?

A. Boston Red Sox.

———◆———

Q. What USC All-American brought his dog Cosmo to every practice session and every home game?

A. Pete Adams.

———◆———

Q. Alyn R. Beals, who signed with the 49ers in 1946, was born in what southern California community?

A. Marysville.

———◆———

Q. What UCLA basketball player holds the individual record for most steals?

A. Reggie Miller (158, 1984-87).

———◆———

Q. What USC running back became known as the "forgotten" tailback?

A. Clarence Davis (who followed Mike Garrett and O.J. Simpson).

Q. What NFL team selected UCLA running back Gaston Green in the first round of the 1988 draft?

A. Los Angeles Rams.

———◆———

Q. In 1988 what Los Angeles Dodger became the first National League right-handed starter to win the *Sport* World Series MVP Award?

A. Orel Hershiser.

———◆———

Q. What southern California-born player led the All America Football Conference during his rookie season, 1947?

A. Alyn Beal.

———◆———

Q. What USC football player became known as the "Noblest Trojan of Them All"?

A. Morley Drury.

———◆———

Q. Who was head football coach at Loyola (Los Angeles) during 1940-41?

A. Martin ("Marty") Brill.

———◆———

Q. Who became USC's first All-American tailback?

A. Mort Kaer (1926).

———◆———

Q. What was Dodger great Duke Snyder's fine when he strained his arm trying to throw a ball out of the Memorial Coliseum?

A. One day's pay, approximately $245.

Q. USC's 1968-69 football team were given what nickname for their fourth-quarter comebacks?

A. "The Cardiac Kids."

———◆———

Q. What Bruin set a new single-season pass reception record at UCLA in 1988?

A. Mike Farr (66).

———◆———

Q. USC defensive lineman Ed White played for what NFL club, 1969-73?

A. Minnesota Vikings.

———◆———

Q. In 1987 the UCLA Bruins baseball team produced what two first-round draft choices?

A. Alex Sanchez and Billy Haselman.

———◆———

Q. In what years did the UCLA basketball Bruins win back-to-back national championships with 30-0 records?

A. 1971-72 and 1972-73.

———◆———

Q. What Santa Ana-born player was selected by the Cincinnati Bengals on the first round of the 1973 draft?

A. Isaac Curtis.

———◆———

Q. What Los Angeles high school produced major leaguers Bobby Tolan, Willie Crawford, and Brock Davis?

A. Fremont High School.

Q. Who was known as the father of southern California golf?

A. Ed Tufts.

———◆———

Q. Who was UCLA's first football All-American?

A. Kenny Washington (1937-39).

———◆———

Q. What Laker star was the first NBA player to return to his original club after being lost in an expansion draft?

A. Gail Goodrich.

———◆———

Q. Ted Williams graduated from what southern California high school?

A. Herbert Hoover High School, San Diego.

———◆———

Q. San Diego State plays its home football games on what playing field?

A. Jack Murphy Stadium.

———◆———

Q. What record breaking UCLA kicker began the 1956 season with a three-yard punt?

A. Kirk Wilson.

———◆———

Q. The famous bronzed Trojan warrior in the center of the USC campus was a composite of what two USC football players?

A. Russ Saunders (1930 Rose Bowl Player of the Game) and Erny Pinckert.

Q. What Long Beach-born infielder led National League third basemen in double plays in 1963?

A. Bob ("Beetles") Bailey (38).

———◆———

Q. In the closing moments of the 1971 game with Oregon State, what UCLA player hit the winning basket?

A. Sidney Wicks.

———◆———

Q. How many times did San Diego-born golfer Mickey Wright win the U.S. Women's Open championship?

A. Four (1958, 1959, 1961, and 1964).

———◆———

Q. What two UCLA Bruins are the only three-time consensus All-Americans in PAC-10 Conference history?

A. Jerry Robinson (1976-77-78) and Kenny Easley (1978-79-80).

———◆———

Q. In what year did the Brooklyn Dodgers move to Los Angeles?

A. 1958.

———◆———

Q. What former UCLA basketball star took over first baseman duties for the Cleveland Indians in 1971?

A. Chris Chambliss.

———◆———

Q. Where did UCLA quarterback Troy Aikman finish in the balloting for the 1988 Heisman Trophy?

A. Third.

Q. What Anaheim native won the silver medal in women's diving at the 1984 Los Angeles Olympic games?

A. Kelly McCormick.

———◆———

Q. What Long Beach native played for the AAFC, NFL, and AFC during the years 1945-64?

A. Benjamin Agajanian.

———◆———

Q. At the beginning of the 1988-89 season, who ranked as USC's all-time leading rusher?

A. Charles White.

———◆———

Q. What is Lew Alcindor's record at UCLA for most points in one game?

A. 61 (against Washington State, 1967).

———◆———

Q. What La Puente-born catcher signed with the Baltimore Orioles for $85,000 in 1961?

A. Andy Etchebarren.

———◆———

Q. Major league pitcher Dock Ellis attended what southern California college?

A. L.A. Harbor Junior College.

———◆———

Q. How many UCLA players were named to the 1988 first team All-PAC-10 football team?

A. Four: Frank Cornish, Chance Johnson, Carnell Lake, and Darryl Henley.

Q. What San Diego-born infielder with the Cincinnati Reds led the majors in 1965 with 130 RBIs and 32 homeruns?

A. Deron Johnson.

Q. Lew Alcindor (now Kareem Abdul-Jabbar) led UCLA to what win-loss record during his collegiate career?

A. 88-2.

Q. In 1965 who became USC's second 1,000-yard rusher?

A. Mike Garrett (following Morley Drury in 1927).

Q. How many NFL championships have the Los Angeles Rams won?

A. One (1951).

Q. At the onset of the 1989 football season, what teams play in the Los Angeles Memorial Coliseum?

A. Los Angeles Raiders and USC Trojans.

Q. What Los Alamitos-born gymnist won a silver medal in the balance beam event at the 1970 World Championships?

A. Cathy Rigby.

Q. In what year did Pasadena first hold its Tournament of Roses parade?

A. 1890.

Q. What Culver City-born major league shortstop was called "Crazy Horse"?

A. Tim Foli.

———◆———

Q. Who holds the UCLA season record for most rebounds?

A. Bill Walton (506, 1973).

———◆———

Q. Where was Dwight Evans, star of the Boston Red Sox, born?

A. Santa Monica.

———◆———

Q. In what year did the Los Angeles Raiders win the Super Bowl?

A. 1984.

———◆———

Q. Through the 1988-89 season, how many UCLA Bruins have been inducted into the National Football Foundation Hall of Fame?

A. Five: Gary Beban, Tom Fears, Donn Moomaw, Al Sparlis, and Kenny Washington.

———◆———

Q. What former USC football coach played major league baseball for the Yankees, Senators, and Athletics?

A. Jessie Hill.

———◆———

Q. What Visalia native led the National League with a 15-4 pitching record for the 1942 Brooklyn Dodgers?

A. Larry French.

Q. Who is the radio voice of the Los Angeles Lakers?

A. Chick Hearn.

———◆———

Q. Which Dodger pitcher holds the career record for most shutouts?

A. Don Drysdale (49).

———◆———

Q. What San Diego-born tennis pro was the first woman to win the French, Wimbledon, U.S., and Australian championships in one year?

A. Maureen Connolly Brinker (1953).

———◆———

Q. What southern California team is the most profitable franchise in professional sports?

A. Los Angeles Dodgers.

———◆———

Q. How many Rose Bowl wins did USC have while John Robinson was head coach?

A. Three: 1977, 1979, 1980.

———◆———

Q. Major league baseball player Bobby Bonds was born in what California city?

A. Riverside.

———◆———

Q. What former UCLA Bruins played in the 1989 Super Bowl?

A. Randy Cross (San Francisco 49ers) and Max Montoya (Cincinnati Bengals).

Q. The Riviera golf course in Los Angeles is referred to by what other name?

A. Hogan's Alley.

———◆———

Q. Who holds the UCLA season record for consecutive free throws?

A. Henry Bibby (36 in 5 games, 1972).

———◆———

Q. With a capacity of 92,516, what is the largest stadium in the NFL?

A. The Los Angeles Coliseum.

———◆———

Q. UCLA head football coach Terry Donahue is a native of what city?

A. Los Angeles.

———◆———

Q. Who was the National League's Rookie of the Year in 1969?

A. Ted Sizemore (Los Angeles Dodgers).

———◆———

Q. Los Angeles-born Thomas Jesse Fears led NFL receivers with 84 catches for 1,116 yards and 7 touchdowns during what year?

A. 1950.

———◆———

Q. What Los Angeles-born baseball figure was a part of the first trade of major league managers?

A. Joe Gordon.

Q. Who led the 1988 California Angels with 25 homeruns?

A. Brian Downing.

———◆———

Q. Who holds the distinction of being UCLA's all-time leading rusher?

A. Gaston Green.

———◆———

Q. What Long Beach native was the world's first 15-foot pole vaulter?

A. Cornelius ("Dutch") Warmerdam.

———◆———

Q. How much did Jerry Buss pay for the Los Angeles Kings, Los Angeles Lakers, and the Forum when he purchased them from Jack Kent Cooke in 1979?

A. $67.5 million.

———◆———

Q. How many national championships has UCLA won in football?

A. Eight (1928, 1931, 1932, 1962, 1967, 1972, 1974, 1978).

———◆———

Q. What two southern California baseball players tied for the American League lead with 106 bases on balls in 1987?

A. Dwight Evans and Brian Downing.

———◆———

Q. What UCLA All-American became the first head coach for the New Orleans Saints?

A. Thomas Fears.

Q. According to coach John McKay, who was the best athlete ever to play at USC?

A. Mike Garrett.

———◆———

Q. What UCLA basketball duo received the Coach John Wooden Award for MVP in 1985?

A. Reggie Miller and Nigel Miguel.

———◆———

Q. What Los Angeles-born high jumper set a world record in 1972 for 18-year-olds at 7 feet, 3 inches?

A. Dwight Stones.

———◆———

Q. Anaheim Stadium began a new tradition in 1985 with the introduction of what confectionary delight?

A. Cinnamon rolls.

———◆———

Q. Who was head coach of the UCLA Bruins football team during the 1971-73 seasons?

A. Pepper Rodgers.

———◆———

Q. Southern Californian Billie Jean King set an all-time record in 1979 by winning how many Wimbledon titles?

A. Twenty.

———◆———

Q. Where was the Cleveland Indians' pitcher Bob Lemon born on September 22, 1920?

A. San Bernardino.

Q. Who was USC's top running back in 1987?

A. Steven Webster.

———◆———

Q. Former Los Angeles Laker Jerry West was known by what nickname?

A. "Mr. Clutch."

———◆———

Q. Frank Gifford began his football career playing end and tailback at what California secondary school?

A. Bakersfield High School.

———◆———

Q. What George Washington High School (Los Angeles) graduate was named All-Pro halfback in 1952 and 1953?

A. Hugh ("King") McElhenny.

———◆———

Q. UCLA fielded its first football team in what year?

A. 1919.

———◆———

Q. What Rose Bowl game had the largest attendance of any college football game ever?

A. January 1, 1973 (USC vs. Ohio State, 106,869).

———◆———

Q. What Los Angeles sports franchise owner is an ex-college professor with a Ph.D. in biochemistry?

A. Jerry Buss (Lakers).

Q. In 1965 the Kansas City Chiefs traded what San Diego-born defensive back to the Oakland Raiders?

A. David Grayson.

---◆---

Q. What 1984 UCLA women's volleyball standout won the Broderick Award as the nation's outstanding collegiate player?

A. Liz Masakayan.

---◆---

Q. How many UCLA head football coaches were former Bruin players?

A. Three (Bert LaBrucherie, George Dickerson, and Terry Donahue).

---◆---

Q. USC's two-time All-American offensive tackle Ron Yary received what coveted award in 1967?

A. The Outland Trophy.

---◆---

Q. UCLA receivers coach Dave Currey was head coach for seven years (1977-83) at what southern California school?

A. Long Beach State.

---◆---

Q. What 1957-59 USC tackle was known as the "Intellectual Assassin?"

A. Ronald J. Mix.

---◆---

Q. Where was 1965 Heisman Trophy winner John Huarte born?

A. Anaheim.

Q. The Anaheim Amigos were a part of what sports organization?

A. American Basketball Association.

———◆———

Q. United Press International ranked UCLA's football team first in what year?

A. 1954.

———◆———

Q. What San Diego native became the first woman to swim the English Channel?

A. Florence Chadwick (September 11, 1951).

———◆———

Q. What was the UCLA men's basketball record at Pauley Pavilion from 1965 to 1975?

A. 149-2.

———◆———

Q. What college was the first to use the Rose Bowl for home football games?

A. Pasadena City College.

———◆———

Q. Former UCLA trainer and track coach Elvin Drake was known by what nickname?

A. "Ducky."

———◆———

Q. Southern California native Ted Williams ended his career having hit how many major league home runs?

A. 521.

Q. What Seely-born long jumper took the gold medal in the 1948 Olympics at Helsinki?

A. Willie Steele.

◆

Q. Who became the first four-time women's basketball All-American at UCLA?

A. Ann Meyers.

◆

Q. Offensive Brad Budde was the first USC recipient of what prestigious honor in 1979?

A. The Lombardi Award.

◆

Q. Dodger Stadium cost how much to construct?

A. $20 million.

◆

Q. What three members of the 1984 gold medal U.S. Olympic gymnastic team competed at UCLA?

A. Peter Viomak, Mitch Gaylord, and Tim Daggett.

◆

Q. What southern California broadcaster is known for saying, "Holy Toledo"?

A. Bill King (Los Angeles Raiders).

◆

Q. What Los Angeles native set the 400-meter world record in Los Angeles in 1964?

A. Mike Larabee (44.9 seconds).

Q. With what clubs did Los Angeles native Beradino play professional baseball for eleven years?

A. St. Louis Browns, Cleveland Indians, and Pittsburgh Pirates.

———◆———

Q. What Santa Monica-born quarterback played for the New York Giants, 1960-61, and the following year for the New York Titans?

A. Clyde Grosscup.

———◆———

Q. 1968-70 UCLA basketball guard John Vallely was given what nickname by teammates because of his play in big games?

A. "Money Man."

———◆———

Q. What Santa Monica-born American League outfielder had a streak of 191 consecutive errorless games in 1973-74?

A. Dwight Evans.

———◆———

Q. What UCLA football duo was known as the "Blair Pair"?

A. Kermit Johnson and James McAlister.

———◆———

Q. What USC running back was known as the "Diving Dervish"?

A. Sam ("Bam") Cunningham.

———◆———

Q. What Los Angeles sports facility hosted the 1984 Olympic Equestrian events?

A. Santa Anita Park.

Q. What Los Angeles-born runner won the NCAA 440-yard dash in 1971 while at UCLA?

A. John Walton Smith (45.3 seconds).

———◆———

Q. What USC defensive football player was named PAC-10 Player of the Year in 1984?

A. Duane Bickett.

———◆———

Q. What Los Angeles-born former pro football player was also elected to the U.S. House of Representatives in 1970?

A. John F. ("Jack") Kemp.

———◆———

Q. In what year did the USC-Notre Dame football rivalry begin?

A. 1926.

———◆———

Q. Who was UCLA's opponent in the 1954 Rose Bowl game, the first to be broadcast in color?

A. Michigan State.

———◆———

Q. When was the first Rose Bowl game broadcast coast to coast by radio?

A. January 1, 1927.

———◆———

Q. How old was Rolling Hills native Tracy Austin when she defeated Martina Navratilova and Chris Evert to win the 1979 U.S. Open?

A. Sixteen.

Q. 1951 USC tailback Frank Gifford went on to be All-Pro with what NFL team?

A. New York Giants.

———◆———

Q. On August 9, 1988, who became the new center for the Los Angeles Kings?

A. Wayne Gretzky.

———◆———

Q. What Long Beach native was the first pole vaulter to vault 18 feet indoors?

A. Steve Smith, 1972.

———◆———

Q. The Oakland A's were defeated by what team in the 1988 World Series?

A. Los Angeles Dodgers.

———◆———

Q. What Fullerton-born Olympian set the world pole vault record in 1972 at 18 feet, 5¾ inches?

A. Bob Seagren.

———◆———

Q. What Torrance-born wide receiver established an NCAA record for most passes caught in a single game?

A. Rick Eber (20).

———◆———

Q. What nickname was given to Coach Howard Jones' USC football teams?

A. "The Thundering Herd."

Q. What Hoover High School graduate became an All-American at Stanford in 1951?

A. William McColl.

Q. In 1973 what Pasadena-born UCLA Bruin recorded a 27-foot, ½-inch long jump for an all-time college record?

A. James McAlister.

Q. What is the distance around the rim of the Rose Bowl?

A. 2,430 feet.

Q. In what year did USC first field a football team?

A. 1888.

Q. Who was voted National League Manager of the Year in 1988?

A. Dodger manager Tommy Lasorda.

Q. In 1988 what former UCLA three-time All-American was inducted into the GTE/Academic All-America Hall of Fame?

A. Donn Moomaw.

Q. What Long Beach native set the American women's javelin toss record on March 3, 1973 at 205 feet, six inches?

A. Kathy Schmidt.

Q. How many USC coaches have been inducted into the National Football Foundation's College Football Hall of Fame?

A. Two: Howard Jones (1951) and John McKay (1988).

———◆———

Q. Los Angeles-born Haven Moses played football for what California university?

A. San Diego State.

———◆———

Q. What USC sophomore earned a starting position as quarterback at USC after beating Fran Tarkenton and Georgia, 10-7?

A. William Nelson.

———◆———

Q. Who led the UCLA basketball team in scoring during the 1963-64 basketball season?

A. Gail Goodrich.

———◆———

Q. Dodger play-by-play broadcasts are in English and Spanish by what two broadcasters?

A. Vin Scully and Jaime Jarrin.

———◆———

Q. In what year did UCLA move its home football games from the Coliseum to the Rose Bowl?

A. 1982.

———◆———

Q. What National Softball Hall of Famer born in Dinuba pitched 757 winning games and lost 88 in her 23-year career?

A. "Blazing Bertha" Tucker.

Q. Who replaced Mike Murphy as head coach of the Los Angeles Kings?

A. Robbie Ftorek.

———◆———

Q. What USFL team played in the Coliseum, 1983-85?

A. Los Angeles Express.

———◆———

Q. The UCLA Bruins football team practices at what facility?

A. Spaulding Field.

———◆———

Q. In 1985 Dodger Fernando Valenzuela set a major league record for how many consecutive innings without an earned run?

A. 41⅓ innings.

———◆———

Q. What award selected by USC football coaches is presented to the team's Most Valuable Player at the end of each season?

A. The Mike McKeever Memorial Award.

———◆———

Q. 1964 NCAA "Player of the Year" honors were awarded to what UCLA basketball senior?

A. Walt Hazsard.

———◆———

Q. What Culver City-born woman swimmer ranked first in the world in the 400-meter and 1,500-meter freestyle in 1983?

A. Tiffany Cohen.

Q. Who was USC's leading rusher in 1954 and 1955?

A. Jon Arnett.

———————◆———————

Q. What play-by-play announcer is the voice of the Los Angeles Kings?

A. Bob Miller.

———————◆———————

Q. UCLA linebacker Donald Paul played for what pro team, 1948-55?

A. Los Angeles Rams.

———————◆———————

Q. The Theodore Gabrielson Award is given annually to the outstanding player of what legendary football game?

A. USC vs. Notre Dame.

———————◆———————

Q. What San Diego-born Olympic swimmer became the first woman sportscaster on a television network?

A. Donna de Varona.

———————◆———————

Q. Who was the first salaried football coach at USC?

A. Harvey Holmes.

———————◆———————

Q. What former UCLA tackle was named to the All-Time All-Pacific Coast team in 1969?

A. Robert Reinhard.

Q. What legendary coach agreed in 1924 to take the head football coach position at USC, subject to a release by his employer?

A. Notre Dame Coach Knute Rockne.

———◆———

Q. In what year did the UCLA men's soccer team take its first NCAA championship?

A. 1985.

———◆———

Q. In the early 1900s, the nickname "Trojans" was given to USC by what person?

A. Owen R. Bird, *Los Angeles Times* sportswriter.

———◆———

Q. What Los Angeles-born sports figure joined the Los Angeles Rams as publicity director in 1947 and later rose to general manager?

A. Texas ("Tex") Schramm.

———◆———

Q. How many PAC-8 titles did Coach John McKay's football teams win during his 16 years at USC?

A. Nine.

———◆———

Q. The UCLA men's golf team captured their first NCAA title in what year?

A. 1988.

———◆———

Q. Who owns the Los Angeles Rams football team?

A. Georgia Frontiere.

Q. What Bakersfield-born Stanford linebacker was All-American in 1971 before joining the Minnesota Vikings?

A. Jeff Siemon.

———◆———

Q. Who was USC's leading pass receiver in 1987?

A. Eric Affholter (44 catches, 4 touchdowns).

———◆———

Q. What Riverside-born woman swimmer set a world record 200 meters in 1:58:23 in 1979?

A. Cynthia ("Sippy") Woodhead.

———◆———

Q. In 1987 what UCLA Trojan threw the most touchdown passes in a single season?

A. Rodney Peete (21).

———◆———

Q. Where did UPI and AP rank UCLA in the final 1988 football polls?

A. Sixth.

———◆———

Q. USC quarterback Irvine ("Cotton") Warburton (1932-34) was born in what California city?

A. San Diego.

———◆———

Q. What Colton-born women's volleyball player became captain of the U.S. team in 1980?

A. Sue Woodstra.

Q. USC's 1937 pole vaulters William Sefton and Earle Meadows were known by what nickname?

A. "Heavenly Twins."

———◆———

Q. Who received PAC-10 football Coach of the Year honors in 1987?

A. USC's Larry Smith.

———◆———

Q. Gene Washington, who led the NFL in reception yards (1,100, 1970) and touchdowns (12, 1972), attended what California secondary school?

A. Long Beach Poly High School.

———◆———

Q. How many USC football players were drafted into the NFL following the 1952 season?

A. Fifteen.

———◆———

Q. What was the UCLA football record for the 1988 season?

A. 10-2.

———◆———

Q. What coach has the highest winning percentage of any in USC's football history?

A. Elmer C. Henderson (45-7, .865).

———◆———

Q. What Seal Beach native took the gold medal in women's platform and springboard diving at the 1952 and 1956 Olympics?

A. Pat McCormick.

Q. What two USC Trojans received Rose Bowl Player of the Game honors in 1975?

A. Pat Haden and Johnny McKay.

———◆———

Q. Who did UCLA defeat, 17-3, in the January 2, 1989, Cotton Bowl?

A. Arkansas.

———◆———

Q. In 1956 what California-born New York Giants running back won the Jim Thorpe Trophy as the NFL's Most Valuable Player?

A. Frank Gifford.

———◆———

Q. What Los Angeles-born second baseman set a major league record in 1950 for most doubles in a doubleheader with eight?

A. Bobby Doerr.

———◆———

Q. The San Diego Padres won their first World Series berth in what year?

A. 1984.

———◆———

Q. What two USC Trojans captained the 1973 football team?

A. Lynn Swann and Artimus Parker.

———◆———

Q. What Anaheim native won over 650 tennis titles during her career?

A. Elizabeth Ryan.

Q. What linebacker was USC's first three-year All-American football player?

A. Richard Wood.

———◆———

Q. What former Los Angeles Athletic Club swimmer and 1939 free style national champion was known as the "Million Dollar Mermaid"?

A. Esther Williams.

———◆———

Q. What San Diego native was the top-rated long jumper in the world in 1971?

A. Arnie Robinson.

———◆———

Q. How many former Trojans played in the 1984 (XVIII) Super Bowl?

A. Three: Marcus Allen, Rod Martin, Don Mosebar (all with the Raiders).

———◆———

Q. Who coached USC baseball from 1942 to 1986?

A. Rod Dedeaux.

———◆———

Q. The Los Angeles Memorial Coliseum hosted what events of the 1984 Olympics?

A. The opening and closing ceremonies and track and field events.

———◆———

Q. What is the name of USC's beautiful white horse mascot?

A. Traveler.

Q. Through the 1988-89 season, how many times has UCLA placed number one on the *USA Today* National Collegiate All-Sports survey?

A. Four.

———◆———

Q. Following his USC career, All-American Mike Garrett starred for what NFL teams?

A. Kansas City Chiefs and San Diego Chargers.

———◆———

Q. San Bernardino native Bob Lemon played a total of 15 years for what major league club?

A. Cleveland Indians.

———◆———

Q. Where did the UCLA men's volleyball team finish in season play for 1988-89?

A. First.

———◆———

Q. USC football coach Elmer Henderson was best known by what nickname?

A. "Gloomy Gus."

———◆———

Q. What Inglewood-born women's volleyball player was voted Best Hitter at the 1981 World Cup Games in Tokyo?

A. Flo Hyman.

———◆———

Q. What costume was Richard Saukko wearing when he first rode USC's white horse mascot in 1961?

A. Charlton Heston's costume from *Ben Hur.*

Q. What California native was the first shot putter to break the 60-foot barrier in 1954?

A. Parry O'Brien (60 feet, 5¼ inches).

———◆———

Q. In 1981-82, what California school became the first to win five NCAA championships?

A. UCLA (men's swimming, men's tennis, men's volleyball, women's softball, and women's track).

———◆———

Q. USC first appeared in the Rose Bowl in what year?

A. 1923 (defeating Penn State, 14-3).

———◆———

Q. What is the largest football stadium in use by the NCAA?

A. The Rose Bowl.

———◆———

Q. The Sullivan Award, presented to the nation's top amateur athlete, has been awarded to what three USC athletes?

A. Diver Sammy Lee (1953), shot putter Parry O'Brien (1959), and swimmer John Naber (1977).

———◆———

Q. What four teammates of the UCLA Bruins men's volleyball squad were also members of the 1988 U.S. Olympic Gold Medal team?

A. Karch Kiraly, Doug Partie, Ricci Luyties, and Dave Saunders.

———◆———

Q. Who became USC's first football All-American in 1925?

A. Brice Taylor.

Q. What California member of the Helms Hall of Fame for fencing was the U.S.'s first woman Olympic fencer?

A. York Romary (Mexico City, 1968).

———◆———

Q. California native Benjamin Agajanian was known by what nickname?

A. "Automatic."

———◆———

Q. At the beginning of the 1989 season, USC had won how many national baseball championships?

A. Eleven.

———◆———

Q. What southern California-born women's golf pro was named Rookie of the Year and Player of the Year in 1978?

A. Nancy Lopez.

———◆———

Q. What major league team did California native Del Crandall manage following his playing career?

A. Milwaukee Brewers and Seattle Mariners.

———◆———

Q. What women's tennis champion was born in Long Beach, November 22, 1943?

A. Billie Jean King.

———◆———

Q. What USC tailback was college football's first 2,000-yard rusher?

A. Marcus Allen.

Q. What UCLA women's basketball star scored 3,198 points during her 1977-81 collegiate career?

A. Denise Curry.

◆

Q. How many Heisman Trophy winners played for USC?

A. Four: Mike Garrett (1965), O.J. Simpson (1968), Charles White (1979), and Marcus Allen (1981).

◆

Q. What former Los Angeles Laker became the sixth man in NBA history to score 20,000 points?

A. Jerry West.

◆

Q. After playing outfield for the Boston Red Sox for 15 years, Dwight Evans changed to what position?

A. First base.

◆

Q. In what year was Elizabeth Ryan inducted into the International Tennis Hall of Fame?

A. 1972.

◆

Q. In what year was Dodger pitcher Don Drysdale elected to the Baseball Hall of Fame?

A. 1984.

◆

Q. What USC quarterback was a Heisman Trophy candidate in 1988?

A. Rodney Peete.

SCIENCE & NATURE

C H A P T E R   S I X

Q. Approximately how many acres of Santa Barbara County are devoted to vineyards?

A. 11,000.

———◆———

Q. What is the largest jet/missile/space vehicle test center in the United States?

A. Edwards Air Force Base.

———◆———

Q. The avocado is a member of what tree family?

A. Laurel.

———◆———

Q. From July until fall, what is the average coastal water temperature of the Pacific Ocean in the Los Angeles area?

A. Approximately 67 degrees Fahrenheit.

———◆———

Q. What area of southern California is called the "Flower Seed Capital of the World"?

A. Lompoc Valley.

Q. At what Edwards Air Force Base facility do space shuttles land?

A. NASA Dryden.

———◆———

Q. A polar orbit launch facility is part of what military base near Lompoc?

A. Vandenberg Air Force Base.

———◆———

Q. During the summer months, what is the most commonly sighted whale off the California coast?

A. Finback, or fin whale.

———◆———

Q. One of the world's largest deposits of what kind of fossils is in the western area of the Santa Ynez Mountains?

A. Diatomaceous earth.

———◆———

Q. What is the city flower of Carlsbad?

A. Bird-of-Paradise.

———◆———

Q. How many tons could a Twenty Mule Team borax wagon carry?

A. Twelve.

———◆———

Q. The Rand Mining District around Randsburg was named for what famous mining area in South Africa?

A. Witwatersrand.

Q. How many types of plants are on display at the University of California, Riverside, Botanic Garden?

A. Over 3,000.

———◆———

Q. What gas is used to treat greenish skinned oranges to help bring out the orange color?

A. Ethylene.

———◆———

Q. In order to produce tungston for World War I, what mineral was mined at Atolia?

A. Scheelite.

———◆———

Q. The Ballistics Missile Office at Norton Air Force Base developed what controversial U.S. defense project?

A. MX missile.

———◆———

Q. A rich deposit of what precious metal was found at Red Mountain in 1919?

A. Silver.

———◆———

Q. What is the weight of the 200-inch Hale telescope of the Palomar Observatory?

A. 500 tons.

———◆———

Q. The spongy part of the orange rind contains what jelling substance?

A. Pectin.

Q. Four thousand units of what kind of machine are used to generate electricity north and west of Mojave?

A. Wind generators.

———◆———

Q. Who, on July 26, 1899, brought in the first Kern County oil well?

A. James and Jonathan Elwood.

———◆———

Q. In December 1986 what aircraft left Edwards Air Force Base on the first non-stop, non-refueled, around-the-world flight?

A. Voyager.

———◆———

Q. What Rosamond company is the only firm west of the Mississippi that manufactures carbon and synthetic graphite?

A. Great Lakes Carbon Corporation.

———◆———

Q. What is the California state reptile?

A. California desert tortoise.

———◆———

Q. The Salton Sea is approximately how much saltier than the Pacific Ocean?

A. Ten percent.

———◆———

Q. John Lang, an early Santa Clarita Valley settler, is credited with having killed a grizzly bear of what record weight?

A. 2,350 pounds.

Q. What sandstone outcroppings between Mint Canyon and Acton are named for a notorious 1800s Mexican bandit?

A. Vasquez Rocks (for Tiburcio Vasquez).

———◆———

Q. What is the length of the Los Angeles Aqueduct?

A. 338 miles.

———◆———

Q. Pico #4 became the first successful commerical oil well in California in September 1876 when redrilled by whom?

A. C. A. ("Alex") Mentry.

———◆———

Q. What three major varieties of avocados are grown in southern California?

A. Hass, Fuerte, and Zutano.

———◆———

Q. Where is California's oldest grape harvest festival held?

A. Rancho Cucamonga.

———◆———

Q. Imperial County's Painted Gorge is situated in what mountain range?

A. Coyote.

———◆———

Q. Where is the Moorten Botanical Gardens?

A. Palm Springs.

Q. What Riverside facility features Dinosaur Day every Saturday?

A. Jurupa Cultural Center.

Q. What is the diameter of the General Sherman sequoia tree's trunk at its base?

A. 36½ feet.

Q. Gray whales migrating along the California coast travel about how many nautical miles per day?

A. 60 to 80.

Q. "Bryce Canyon in Miniature" is the nickname applied to what southern California natural attraction?

A. Red Rock Canyon.

Q. What is the name of Bakersfield's combined zoo, botanical garden, and natural history museum?

A. CLAM.

Q. Sweet peas grown in southern California's flower-seed industry produce approximately how many pounds of seed per acre?

A. 700 to 800.

Q. Approximately how many acres of California land are devoted to the production of oranges?

A. 250,000.

Q. What is Riverside's "downtown mountain"?

A. Mount Rubidoux.

———◆———

Q. What Redlands firm evolved into Lockheed Propulsion?

A. Grand Central Rocket.

———◆———

Q. How long is the Salton Sea?

A. 35 miles.

———◆———

Q. What southern California community is called the "Carrot Capital of the World"?

A. Holtville.

———◆———

Q. In what part of the Kern County Museum may children enjoy "hands-on" displays?

A. Lori Brock Junior Museum.

———◆———

Q. Where in the Imperial Valley is the Tomato Festival held each year?

A. Niland.

———◆———

Q. What was the weight of the record orange mouth corvina pulled from the Salton Sea in 1988?

A. 36 pounds.

Q. How many species of cactus are native to California?

A. Four.

--- ◆ ---

Q. What rare type of horses are bred at Fairmont Farms, Solvang?

A. Andalusian.

--- ◆ ---

Q. In what year was Santa Barbara's giant Moreton Bay fig tree, largest of its kind in the U.S., planted?

A. 1877.

--- ◆ ---

Q. During the late 1800s and early 1900s, what mineral water bottler and salesman made Spring Valley water internationally famous?

A. Alfred Huntington Isham.

--- ◆ ---

Q. "Green gold" is a term applied to what southern California fruit crop?

A. Avocados.

--- ◆ ---

Q. How many of the ten largest oil fields in the U.S. are in Kern County?

A. Four.

--- ◆ ---

Q. On what Santa Monica Mountains trail are visitors able to view plants, animals, and minerals utilized by the Chumash and Tongva Indians?

A. Satwiwa Loop Trail.

Q. Joshua Tree National Monument covers how many acres?

A. 558,000.

───────◆───────

Q. Situated north of Landers and weighing an estimated 23,000 tons, what is the world's largest solitary bolder?

A. Giant Rock.

───────◆───────

Q. Drilled in 1914, the main Ventura oil field produced how many barrels of oil per day at its peak?

A. 90,000.

───────◆───────

Q. The Whittier Citrus Association, formed in 1901, started shipping fruit under what label?

A. "Quaker Brand."

───────◆───────

Q. What vegetable packing company is the largest manufacturing firm in Blythe?

A. Hi-Value Processors.

───────◆───────

Q. "City of Trees" is the nickname given to what southern California community?

A. Whittier.

───────◆───────

Q. Who was the first person to advocate bringing Colorado River water to Los Angeles?

A. Harriet Russell Strong.

Q. What four types of fish are found in the Salton Sea?

A. Orange mouth corvina, sargo, gulf croaker, and tilapia.

◆

Q. In agricultural production, where does Kern County rank in relationship to all other counties in the state?

A. Third.

◆

Q. What Inyo County peak received its name for its sanguine coloration?

A. Dripping Blood Mountain.

◆

Q. In 1903 what new species of trout was discovered in a tributary of the Kern River?

A. *Salmo roosevelti* (discovered by Dr. B. W. Evermann).

◆

Q. What is California's second most important citrus fruit?

A. Lemon.

◆

Q. Who in 1911 discovered that drained peat lands in Orange County were capable of growing celery?

A. D. E. Smeltzer.

◆

Q. In what year was alfalfa introduced to California?

A. 1854.

Q. What Carlsbad floriculturalist became known as the "Father of the Bird-of-Paradise"?

A. Clint Pedley.

———◆———

Q. The common Sultana grape of the late 1800s and early 1900s was replaced in the table grape market by what variety?

A. Thompson Seedless.

———◆———

Q. Where on May 1, 1947, was radar for commercial and private planes first demonstrated?

A. Culver City.

———◆———

Q. What two deserts meet in the Joshua Tree National Monument?

A. Mojave and Colorado.

———◆———

Q. On October 14, 1947, who became the first person to fly beyond the speed of sound in the Bell X-1 rocket plane?

A. Charles ("Chuck") Yeager.

———◆———

Q. What is the city flower of Fullerton?

A. Carnation.

———◆———

Q. In 1910 what distinctly American disease was first recognized in Tulare County?

A. Tularemia (rabbit fever).

Q. Where on April 11, 1941, was the first hydrogen-cooled outdoor turbine electric generator put into operation?

A. Glendale.

———◆———

Q. What unique bird raising facility was opened at South Pasadena in 1886?

A. Ostrich farm.

———◆———

Q. The Shoshonean word for sheep is applied to what Death Valley National Monument peak?

A. Tucki Mountain.

———◆———

Q. What per unit price tag was placed on the Northrop Corporation's radar evading B-2 Stealth bomber?

A. $530 million.

———◆———

Q. In what year did the California Date Association establish its first packing plant at Indio?

A. 1918.

———◆———

Q. The fruit of what plant is sometimes referred to as a "beach apple"?

A. Prickly pear cactus.

———◆———

Q. Also called Paiute Monument, what Inyo County granite monolith honors a Paiute medicine man?

A. Winnedumah.

Q. What city is the home of the California Institute of Technology?

A. Pasadena.

Q. In 1980 what five islands were designated as the Channel Islands National Park?

A. Anacapa, San Miguel, Santa Barbara, Santa Cruz, and Santa Rosa.

Q. What is the largest natural harbor in southern California?

A. San Diego Bay.

Q. Where may the Tegelberg Cactus Gardens be viewed?

A. Lucerne Valley.

Q. What is the largest source of water for most communities in Victor Valley?

A. Mojave River.

Q. Botanists from the University of California, Riverside, have discovered what bush thought to be the oldest living plant?

A. A creosote bush.

Q. Kern County is the world's largest producer of what mineral?

A. Borax.

Q. What is the largest vegetable cash crop in Imperial County?

A. Lettuce.

Q. In what year did Bakersfield acquire electricity?

A. 1900.

Q. What ten-acre meditation gardens area is situated in Pacific Palisades?

A. Self-Realization Fellowship Lake Shrine.

Q. Providing a genetic pool for big cats, where is the Exotic Feline Breeding Compound?

A. Rosamond.

Q. Near what community is the Desert Tortoise Natural Area?

A. California City.

Q. With 38 miles of shoreline, what is the largest freshwater lake in southern California?

A. Lake Isabella.

Q. What was the most famous gold mine in the Rand Mining District northeast of Mojave?

A. Yellow Aster Mine.

Q. As a traditional celebration of spring, where is the Lilac Festival held each year in Kern County?

A. Frazier Park, Pine Mountain Community.

◆

Q. Prehistoric animal skeletons from the Rancho La Brea Tar Pits are displayed in what facility?

A. George C. Page Museum.

◆

Q. What natural area north of Barstow is noted for its wealth of 12 to 14 million-year-old land mammal fossils?

A. Rainbow Basin.

◆

Q. What 1.4-million-acre site was designated as the nation's first National Scenic Area in 1980?

A. East Mojave National Scenic Area.

◆

Q. The Mojave yucca is a member of what plant family?

A. Lily.

◆

Q. What was the only California project undertaken by archaeologist/paleontologist Dr. Louis S. B. Leakey?

A. Calico Early Man Archaeological Site.

◆

Q. Situated east of Barstow, what is the largest sun-generated power plant in the world?

A. Solar One.

Q. The Imperial Sand Dunes near Glamis are known by what nickname?

A. "America's Sahara."

---◆---

Q. How far below sea level is the Imperial Valley?

A. 52 feet.

---◆---

Q. A burst canal dike on what river created the Salton Sea between 1905 and 1907?

A. Colorado.

---◆---

Q. What beachfront landscaped preserve at Santa Barbara protects fowl?

A. Andree Clark Bird Refuge.

---◆---

Q. What is the average amount of rainfall annually at Blythe?

A. 3.96 inches.

---◆---

Q. For what purpose did the Santa Fe Railroad plant 4,000 acres of eucalyptus trees at Rancho Santa Fe in the early 1900s?

A. Railroad ties.

---◆---

Q. What seaside community, known as the "Natural Home of the Avocado," sponsored Avocado Days annually from 1925 until World War II?

A. Carlsbad.

Q. What southern California floriculturalist became famous for developing new colors of watsonias?

A. E. P. Zimmerman.

———◆———

Q. How long is Santa Catalina Island?

A. 21 miles.

———◆———

Q. What is the rarest tree in California?

A. Catalina mahogany.

———◆———

Q. Where is the only resident population of bald eagles in southern California?

A. Santa Catalina Island.

———◆———

Q. In whose honor is the 37-acre botanical garden near Avalon named?

A. William Wrigley, Jr.

———◆———

Q. On March 10, 1933, what natural disaster took many lives and almost leveled Compton?

A. An earthquake.

———◆———

Q. The San Diego Wild Animal Park, featuring some 2,500 animals, covers how many acres?

A. 1,800.

Q. At 11,049 feet, what is Death Valley National Monument's highest mountain?

A. Telescope Peak.

———◆———

Q. The valley floor of Death Valley is how many feet below sea level?

A. 282.

———◆———

Q. What is the average temperature of the water at Tecopa Hot Springs Park?

A. 103 degrees Fahrenheit.

———◆———

Q. What fruit common to southern California is known by such names as "alligator pear," "laurel peach," "vegetable marrow," and "Spanish pear"?

A. Avocado.

———◆———

Q. How long is the All-American Canal?

A. 85 miles.

———◆———

Q. What is the largest inland sea on the North American continent?

A. Salton Sea.

———◆———

Q. What southern California county ranks first in the nation for pen-fed cattle?

A. Imperial.

Q. By the late 1970s, breeding colonies of what large seals were re-established on some of the Channel Islands?

A. Elephant seals.

———◆———

Q. The Jacaranda is the city tree of what southern California community?

A. Fullerton.

———◆———

Q. The official city flag of Gardena features the branches of what type of tree in its design?

A. Bonsai.

———◆———

Q. What is the body temperature of a sea otter?

A. 100 degrees Fahrenheit.

———◆———

Q. Completed in 1982, what became the world's first utility-scale solar electric power plant?

A. ARCO Solar Photovoltaia Power Plant.

———◆———

Q. What 1,200-acre park at Palm Desert features exotic wildlife and 1,500 varieties of plant life?

A. The Living Desert.

———◆———

Q. What variety of palm tree is most common along the fifteen-mile length of Palm Canyon?

A. *Washingtonia filifera.*

Q. What endangered species of bird has been found to nest in secluded sections of Murray Canyon?

A. Least Bell's vireo.

———◆———

Q. In what valley are 95 percent of the nation's dates grown?

A. Coachella Valley.

———◆———

Q. What term is applied to people who grow, prune, and harvest date trees?

A. Palmeros.

———◆———

Q. How many species of owls are found in the San Jacinto Wildlife Area?

A. Six.

———◆———

Q. Measuring almost two feet in length, the roadrunner is a member of what bird family?

A. Cuckoo.

———◆———

Q. What is the state flower of California?

A. Golden Poppy.

———◆———

Q. What desert rodent noted for jumping around on its powerful hind legs does not have to drink water to survive?

A. Kangaroo rat.

Q. In what year was the Upper Newport Bay Reserve purchased by the state of California for the Department of Fish and Game?

A. 1975.

Q. With a wingspan of up to 55 inches, what is the largest variety of owl in California?

A. Great horned owl.

Q. What is the California state bird?

A. California Valley quail.

Q. In ancient times the Imperial Valley was part of what body of water?

A. The Gulf of Baja California.

Q. What California wildlife area is completely below sea level?

A. Imperial Wildlife Area.

Q. On July 17, 1989, what two pilots took the B-2 Stealth bomber on its maiden flight?

A. Col. Richard Couch and Bruce J. Hinds.

Q. In 1887 who brought Algerian date shoots to Indio that were used to develop California's date industry?

A. C. P. Huntington, president of the Southern Pacific Railroad.

Q. What is the average weight of an adult coyote?

A. 25 to 30 pounds.

———◆———

Q. On May 3, 1989, what sex change pioneer died in San Clemente?

A. Christine Jorgensen.

———◆———

Q. Where in 1896 were California's first successful off-shore oil wells drilled?

A. Summerland.

———◆———

Q. What type of commerical communication service to Los Angeles was inaugurated on July 16, 1920?

A. Radio telephone.

———◆———

Q. In what year was the last report of a grizzly bear shot in Tulare County?

A. 1922.

———◆———

Q. A California sea lion in captivity consumes how many pounds of fish per day?

A. 15 to 20.

———◆———

Q. In 1976 what vessel was sunk in Santa Monica Bay to become California's first Liberty ship artificial reef?

A. U.S.S. *Palawan*.

Q. With its termination point at Perris Lake in Riverside County, what has been called the "longest fishing hole this side of the ocean"?

A. The California Aqueduct.

---◆---

Q. On September 25, 1890, what became the nation's second national park?

A. Sequoia National Park.

---◆---

Q. Though rarely seen, what is the largest animal in the Joshua Tree National Monument?

A. Desert bighorn sheep.

---◆---

Q. What planetarium is near Santa Barbara's Museum of Natural History?

A. Gladwin Planetarium.

---◆---

Q. What 164-foot cascade is near Solvang?

A. Nojoqui Falls.

---◆---

Q. Some of the bristle cone pines in Inyo County are of what age?

A. 4,000 years old.

---◆---

Q. What fracture in the earth's crust stretches the full length of southern California and on to the northwest?

A. San Andreas Fault.

Q. With the addition of four new chicks hatched at the San Diego Wild Animal Park, the population of California condors rose to what number in 1989?

A. 32.

———◆———

Q. What term is used for dense thickets of chamise, manzanita, scrub oak, and wild lilac in arid areas of southern California?

A. Chaparral.

———◆———

Q. With wingspans of 8½ to 10 feet, what is the largest land bird on the North American continent?

A. California condor.

———◆———

Q. In what year were California's first state-wide game laws enacted?

A. 1854.

———◆———

Q. Where was California's first "production model" artificial reef completed for public fishing in 1960?

A. Santa Monica Bay.

———◆———

Q. What southern California community bears the title of "Avocado Capital of the World"?

A. Escondido.

———◆———

Q. Who operates the Palomar Observatory?

A. California Institute of Technology.

Q. What was the first gold mine to start operation in the Julian area?

A. George Washington Mine.

———◆———

Q. Southern California's some 200,000 date palms produce approximately how many pounds of fruit annually?

A. 40 million.

———◆———

Q. In 1944 what top security experimental aircraft became the nation's first military rocket plane?

A. Northrop's MX-324 "Rocket Wing."

———◆———

Q. Reaching lengths of 15 to 16 feet, what is the average weight of adult male elephant seals?

A. 4,000 to 5,000 pounds.

———◆———

Q. What California marine mammal often uses a rock positioned on its chest to break open hard mollusk shells?

A. Sea otter.

———◆———

Q. How many farmers started the Los Angeles Farmers Market during the Great Depression of the 1930s?

A. 18.

———◆———

Q. What park overlooks Santa Monica Bay?

A. Palisades Park.

Q. For its size, what is the first all-new zoo to have been built in modern times?

A. The Los Angeles Zoo.

———————◆———————

Q. What was the first gyro-stabilized American oceanliner?

A. *Mariposa* (sailed from Los Angeles, October 26, 1956).

———————◆———————

Q. What giant tree native to California is named for the inventor of the Cherokee written alphabet?

A. Sequoia (for Sequoya).

———————◆———————

Q. Such geological wonders as the Painted Gorge, Petrified Forest, and Fossil Oyster Beds are in the southwestern corner of what county?

A. Imperial.

———————◆———————

Q. What large state park covers most of the eastern third of San Diego County?

A. Anza-Borrego Desert State Park.

———————◆———————

Q. The Cholla Cactus Garden is in what national monument?

A. Joshua Tree National Monument.

———————◆———————

Q. At 14,494 feet, what is the highest point in California?

A. Mount Whitney.

Q. What record high temperature for the U.S. was recorded in Death Valley on July 10, 1913?

A. 134 degrees Fahrenheit.

———◆———

Q. In what year were borax deposits discovered in Death Valley?

A. 1873.

———◆———

Q. What crater is situated at the northern end of the Death Valley National Monument?

A. Ubehebe Crater.

———◆———

Q. What 3,500-year-old sequoia is the world's largest tree in terms of volume of wood?

A. "General Sherman."

———◆———

Q. What name was given to the young gray whale kept at San Diego's Sea World, March 1971 to March 1972?

A. Gigi.

———◆———

Q. How many rose bushes fill the Sunken Garden at Exposition Park, Los Angeles?

A. 16,000.

———◆———

Q. Where is the California Museum of Science and Industry?

A. Los Angeles.

Q. The Rancho La Brea Tar Pits are situated in what Los Angeles park?

A. Handcock Park.

Q. The Sequoia National Park is situated on the western slopes of what mountain range?

A. Sierra Nevada.

Q. What national monument on Point Loma is known for its tidal pools and nearby whales to watch?

A. Cabrillo National Monument.

Q. What are the two best months to enjoy the colorful wild-flowers of the Santa Monica Mountains National Recreation Area?

A. March and April.

Q. First flight-tested at Muroc Dry Lake in 1940, what was truly the first American flying wing aircraft?

A. The Northrop N1M "Jeep."

Q. What world famous marine research facility is at La Jolla?

A. Scripps Institution of Oceanography.

Q. The Rancho Santa Anna Botanic Gardens are exclusively devoted to what type of plants?

A. Those native to California.

SCIENCE & NATURE

Q. What sanctuary near Modjeska is operated by California State University at Fullerton?

A. Tucker Wildbird Sanctuary.

◆

Q. What animal is the "trained seal" of circuses and other shows?

A. The California sea lion.

◆

Q. In whose honor is the Salk Institute for Biological Studies named?

A. Dr. Jonas Salk.

◆

Q. What rare type of pine tree grows north of La Jolla?
A. Torrey pines.

◆

Q. Measuring 5½ inches in length, what color is a California condor egg?

A. Pale green.

◆

Q. What California fish hatchery is situated in San Bernardino County?

A. Mojave River hatchery.

◆

Q. What endangered species of bird is known for its buff colored eggs with irregular purple and brown markings?

A. California least tern.

Q. In 1972 where was the only nesting site of the California brown pelican in the entire state?

A. Anacapa Island.

———————◆———————

Q. What is the California state tree?

A. Redwood.

———————◆———————

Q. On May 28, 1931, what aircraft piloted by J. M. Miller ended its trans-continental flight in San Diego?

A. Autogiro.

———————◆———————

Q. At Rogers Dry Lake on May 18, 1953, who became the first woman to pilot an airplane faster than the speed of sound?

A. Jacqueline Cochran.

———————◆———————

Q. Where was the first forest service aerial patrol established on June 1, 1919?

A. Riverside.

———————◆———————

Q. What Pasadena resident patented a submarine jet propulsion device on February 15, 1949?

A. Fritz Zwicky.

———————◆———————

Q. Situated just west of Point Dune, what is Los Angeles' largest county-owned beach?

A. Zuma Beach.

Q. What famous water zoo and oceanarium is situated on the Palos Verdes Peninsula?

A. Marineland.

◆

Q. The San Fernando Valley covers how many square miles?

A. 220.

◆

Q. What La Canada attraction is noted for its vast collection of camellias?

A. Descanso Gardens.

◆

Q. What facility is known for its 100-inch, 100-ton Hooker telescope?

A. Mount Wilson Observatory.

◆

Q. What desert snake is noted for its unusual method of movement?

A. Sidewinder rattlesnake.

◆

Q. Measuring about 16 inches in length, what desert dwelling reptile was sometimes used by Indians as a source of food?

A. Chuckwalla.

◆

Q. What unique head feature distinguishes California and Gambel's species from all other quail?

A. Teardrop topknot.